SELLING
in
TOUGH TIMES

Also by Tom Hopkins

How to Master the Art of Selling

The Official Guide to Success

How to Master the Art of Listing Real Estate

How to Master the Art of Selling Real Estate

Low Profile Selling

Your Guide to Greatness in Selling

Selling for Dummies

Sales Closing for Dummies

Sales Prospecting for Dummies

Mastering the Art of Listing and Selling Real Estate

The Certifiable Salesperson (with Laura Laaman)

*Sell It Today, Sell It Now—The Art of the One-Call Close
(with Pat Leiby)*

Laugh Your Way to Health & Wealth

SELLING
in
TOUGH TIMES

Secrets to Selling When No One Is Buying

TOM HOPKINS

**BUSINESS
PLUS**

NEW YORK   BOSTON

Business Plus
Hachette Book Group
237 Park Avenue
New York, NY 10017

www.HachetteBookGroup.com

Business Plus is an imprint of Grand Central Publishing.
The Business Plus name and logo are trademarks of Hachette Book Group, Inc.

Printed in the United States of America

First Edition: February 2010

10 9 8 7 6 5 4 3 2 1

Library of Congress Cataloging-in-Publication Data

Hopkins, Tom.
    Selling in tough times : secrets to selling when no one is buying / Tom
Hopkins. — 1st. ed.
        p.   cm.
    Includes index.
    ISBN 978-0-446-54814-4
    1. Selling. I. Title.

HF5438.25.H666 2010
658.85—dc22   2009013077

For over thirty years, Tom Hopkins International has been blessed to prosper while serving the needs of salespeople the world over. Because of the commitment and dedication of an incredible team of people, I have been able to write fifteen books, conduct over 4,500 live seminars, and produce countless hours of video and audio instruction on how to sell. I will be forever beholden to and thankful for these wonderful people:

Spencer Price, Chief Financial Officer
Laura Oien, President
Judy Slack, Director of Research & Development
    (and ghost writer)
Kristine Weaver, Office Manager
Linda Hunt, Customer Service
Frank Valenzuela, Warehouse Operations Manager
Sharon Kolacny, Receptionist *Extraordinaire*
Deborah Scroggins, Seminar Manager
    (and my personal assistant)
Rosie Wolfrum, Accounts Receivable
Michael Hansen, Onsite Program Manager

Acknowledgments

I would like to specifically acknowledge "The Millionaire Maker," Dan S. Kennedy, and fellow sales trainer Laura Laaman for their contributions to the book.

And special acknowledgment goes to my editor, Leila Porteous of Grand Central Publishing.

Contents

CONTENTS

Introduction

Some of today's richest and most influential business people got their starts in sales, and now they regularly find themselves on the Forbes 400 Richest Americans list and as leaders of major corporations. And they didn't necessarily earn Champion status or build their fortunes during prime economic times. Rather, many of them found ways to take market share by serving a specific need or by working hard to improve upon what the competition was offering.

To name a few:

Sheldon Adelson, the billionaire leader of the Las Vegas Sands Corporation;

S. Daniel Abraham of Thompson Medical Company (the folks who manufacture and market Slim-Fast products);

Anne Mulcahy, CEO of Xerox;

Richard M. Schulze of Best Buy; and

Philip H. Knight of Nike.

They came to understand that business isn't about products. It's about serving the needs of people. In fact, when you hear the term *market* from now on, I want you to interpret that to mean *people*. When you're selling, you're in the people business. You sell your products and services to people. Therefore, communicating with them and understanding their needs and motivations is what selling is really all about.

While industries, economies, and companies run in cycles, they are all people-dependent. People are dependent upon the companies to offer products and to provide jobs. When any hiccup in business occurs, it's typically going to require change that impacts its people—both the employees and the clients.

Change is one of the most frightening words in the English language for many people. For those who have learned to embrace change, its impact is not as disruptive. For those who want things to stay the same, it can be downright paralyzing. When people become paralyzed with fear, they stop making decisions—especially those involving their security (translated "money").

All businesses run in cycles. There are up cycles, downturns, and everything in between. And you can succeed in any of them. It doesn't really matter all that much what happens in the marketplace when you are a true professional in sales. Your key to success lies within yourself and what you believe about where you currently find yourself on the business cycle. How well you are prepared to respond proactively to each cycle you'll encounter in your long-term career is what this book is all about.

You see, in economic or industry downturns the sales-person's job is more vital than ever. Some consumers won't shop for anything other than necessities in challenging times. It's the salesperson's job to help them recognize their need for and ability to afford other items.

There's a lack of impulse buyers who are usually the gravy for businesses. And the meat-and-potato big clients may be slimming down their orders or spreading them further apart. Again, it falls to the sales team to continue to serve the needs of these big clients and to help them through the tough times so when things turn back around, they remain loyal to you, your brand, and your company.

It's up to the salespeople of the world, those who put their egos on the line every day, to get out there and make things happen. This is the same advice I gave in the para-lyzing days here in the United States after the shock of the attacks on September 11, 2001. It was not meant to diminish the tragedy of what happened on that fateful day, but to do what we do best . . . pick ourselves up and keep moving forward. It's only by doing normal things that a sense of normalcy returns.

You may need to readjust your thinking and some of your strategies to sell yourself out of a slump, but know that it can be done and has been done by millions of sales professionals facing worse disasters than you currently see before you.

Selling can and does continue during tough times. And the true sales professionals who understand and act on what needs to be done not only survive but thrive.

Mastering the art of selling is mastering the art of providing your clients the products, services, and contact after the sale that they want, need, and, more important, deserve. That's how individuals and organizations will ride out the waves and the roller coasters of the future. That's how they'll not only survive any challenge but will thrive on it, prosper with it, and achieve greatness through it.

Believe me. I've ridden that roller coaster and surfed (and survived) the rising and falling waves of change. I know selling. I did physically demanding labor, lugging steel around construction sites, before finding out how exciting the world of selling could be. By investing in myself and in some training I entered the real estate profession. I worked hard to serve as many clients as possible, and I was able to achieve levels of success beyond my wildest dreams. I transitioned into sales training after seeing how many others were like I had been, loving the field of selling but not understanding that it is something to be learned, just like any other skill. Today Tom Hopkins International is recognized as America's premier sales training organization. Please read the words in this book and take them to heart. I know what I'm talking about. I also know that you can take what you learn here to achieve your most cherished goals, and beyond, by providing superior service to your customers through selling.

SELLING
in
TOUGH TIMES

1. What a Selling Career Really Is

The English philosopher Alfred North Whitehead wrote, "The future is big with every possibility of achievement and of tragedy." How we handle those possibilities, and, perhaps more important, how we handle the challenges will determine whether we revel in our own achievement or reap our own tragedy.

Whenever you are faced with tough times, it's time to get busy. The sooner you begin focusing on what's happening and what actions to take to get past it, instead of bemoaning whatever negative event happened, the sooner you can start moving forward on improving today's situation.

That may sound like a supersimplified solution and it is, but what good does it do to moan and groan and talk about how bad things are? In fact, the longer we focus on slow sales, a bad rap in the media, losing a big client, or the scary global economy, the more we prolong their effects by our own inaction.

When we continue to talk about the downside of things, we become part of the problem. We're helping to spread the virus of bad news, just as we'd be spreading any other kind of virus by not washing our hands or covering our mouths when we cough or sneeze. In fact, covering our mouths is the best answer to both mental and physical health when we encounter something that is potentially viral, whether it's truly a virus or just bad news. We need to think, act, and live in the present moment.

Let's face it. If you stay in any type of career long enough, you're bound to run the course of both high cycles and lows. How you handle them depends a lot on what their causes are.

THE CAUSES OF TOUGH TIMES

Demographics

People change. A current and dramatic change in demographics has and will continue to have an enormous impact on the global economy. In the United States one such change is called "the graying of America." In actuality, it's the graying of the entire world's population. If you work in the ever-increasing international market, take note. A vast number of people from the baby boom generation are finding their needs changing. Companies will have to adapt to that approaching tidal wave of change or be swept beneath it.

At the same time, companies need to serve the needs of today's youth when it comes to technology, financial, and consumer goods. While Grandma might not care or even understand that the next version of MP3 players has a time-travel feature, the grandkids who will soon control much of the world's wealth do care. And they care very much.

2

Tough times could get really tough for some companies. Finding, acquiring, and then holding on to good clients will be a major challenge, if not *the* major challenge, for the foreseeable future. But again, there is a way to meet that challenge.

More than ever before, companies and individual suppliers must focus on building organizations and product/service mixes that meet the specialized needs of an incredible variety of individuals and companies.

Economic Cycles

The economy will continue to be volatile. "Of course, Tom, when has it not been volatile?" If anyone develops the ability to accurately predict what will happen in the economy, they will rule the world!

In the early days of this century, we saw phenomenal growth in many service industries. For years you couldn't watch a television news program, read a general-interest magazine, or flip through your local newspaper without reading glowing stories about the real estate boom or the incredible gains in the stock market.

That's great, but as universal law tells us, every boom is followed by a bust and tough times—or, in kinder, gentler terms, a "correction." What goes up must come down. Of course, it (whatever "it" is) will most likely go back up again at the proper moment in the economic cycle.

Only smart business people will be in a position to successfully ride the roller coaster through the bottoming out and the inevitable rise back up to the heights. Companies and the individuals who work inside them will have to position themselves as worthy providers through fast action, a proper product/service mix for their market(s), and by providing genuine and personal service.

Politics

I don't care which political party you support or even if you consider yourself apolitical. Please understand this. You are deeply, heavily, and intimately involved in politics— local, state, and federal. There's no escaping it.

Think not? Think again. Whether you are anti–big government or pro–big government or somewhere in the middle is irrelevant. Government—politics—is a major factor in the success or failure of your business, in the achievement of your goals, and in the process of securing a safe, sound, and happy future.

Many industries have been under intense scrutiny by local, state, and federal regulators and governing bodies. This trend will continue as long as there are unscrupulous and greedy people in both leadership and sales positions.

A key element of what goes on in business involves ethics. Think of the very prominent scandals that have rocked the business world in years past. The Savings & Loan operations of the 1980s. Insider trading. Worldcom. Tyco. ImClone Systems (Martha Stewart). Enron.

Because of the fallout from some of these scandals, people in the highest positions in business are now being held accountable. The bottom line of many of these failures (of businesses and the people who run them) often seems to boil down to greed and/or having poor ethical standards.

4

To prevent a future mass violation of business practices, every one of us needs to step up and make the term *accountability* predominant in our mission statements. One of the best books I've ever seen on this topic is John G. Miller's *QBQ! The Question Behind the Question. QBQ!* is practical, universal, and timeless because personal accountability applies to people and organizations no matter what's going on. We'll talk more about your personal ethics and how they will impact your survival rate later in this chapter.

Currently business regulation is intense on all levels. It will only get more complex as the years roll by. Increased regulation and government monitoring will heighten the risk of losing your job, your income, and even your business. Failure to understand and comply with the ever-increasing burden of regulations could be disastrous. The costs of noncompliance, the loss of reputation, the loss of a sound customer base, and the risk of offering poor or poorly targeted products and services could devastate any business.

I have always practiced and promoted sticking to the highest possible standards of business practice. If the typical standards in your industry are low, don't give in to them. Raise the bar. Adhering to the highest ethical standards will be essential to developing and maintaining customer loyalty—the foundation of all success. Especially during challenging times you must be a shining example of sound moral values. Stay close to your client base and help them through these times, and they'll stay with you long-term.

Technology

The waves of change continue to roll in as new technologies provide better means to offer improved and more personal service at more affordable rates. Yet, as with everything else, implementing technological change has its pluses and minuses. You need to analyze any change you're considering in how you do business against the end result for your clients.

Why should a potential client trudge downtown or have a salesperson violate the personal space of their home, when in the same amount of time they can shop half a dozen or more organizations online? We know the answer is because salespeople are industry experts, and unless the client is interested in investing the same amount of time you do in learning your business, they're not likely to make decisions that are truly good for them. But few consumers understand that.

Why does John or Joan Consumer need to dress up, drive the car, fight traffic, and wait in line to make a purchase when they can sit in their home, sipping coffee in their bathrobes, and conclude a purchase with the tapping of their fingers on a keyboard?

Why indeed?

The solution can be found in the challenge. Technology can be easy. People can come to believe they don't need you—the salesperson. If your Web site tells a client everything you would tell them, you can make yourself obsolete—except for the fact that not many Web sites offer personalized service. They can't do analyses of which product best suits a client's true needs now while considering that client's needs for the future.

Technology is great, but only when used as an accessory to genuine personal service targeted to solving each client's individual challenges.

Industry

There have been times, and there will continue to be times, when certain industries suffer. A few that come to mind in my lifetime are the time-share industry, the real estate and mortgage industries, the automotive industry, and credit-related services. They have all taken some pretty hard hits. In some cases they have had to police themselves to cure indiscretions and reinvent themselves to stay strong in providing services that are very much needed and wanted by consumers but not offered the way they were.

Mother Nature

If you live along any shoreline in our country, you could very well take on a storm serious enough to shut down business for quite some time. Inlanders face tornado season annually. Certain parts of our country are more prone to wildfires than others. And large snowfalls have been known to bring the world to a halt in other parts of our country.

When Mother Nature gets rolling, we all need to stop, manage the most basic of necessities, and slow down until these things pass and we all recover. Then, we pick up the pieces and move forward, don't we? We *are* a resilient lot, and most often we will come back stronger and better. It just may take a little time.

Competition

If you don't watch your competition so you can be ready to counter their moves, you'll soon find yourself sliding down the list of top companies in your industry. When a young start-up wants to be a new player in the world of established business, they may make some product offers that your company simply cannot beat or even come close to matching.

If you're not prepared, you'll be blindsided by—and could find yourself in a very embarrassing situation with—a long-term client who expects you to know the story behind this incredible new offer. If you try to avoid it, or if you hope they won't bring up the challenge and they do so late in the sales process, your admission of knowledge only after they ask about it will make you appear weak or as trying to hide or sidestep the issue.

Competition can also heat up as clients pit you against others in your industry to get the most for their money and to get the most economical offering available. If you offer a higher-end and higher-quality product that's not the most economical, you need to be prepared to bring it up and brag about that concern early in your presentations. Timing is everything, and if you're operating from an offensive position when it comes to a potential concern, the client will see you as well-prepared and knowledgeable.

Personal

Many of us have encountered times in our lives when personal situations had a negative impact on our business lives. Some were due to our own mishandling of matters. Others, like a major illness of our own or that of a close family member, take priority over what we do for a living. Being human, we have limitations. There is only so much we can bear, and there will be times when business just has to take a backseat until we get back on our feet. As with any other challenge, we need to handle it as best we can and keep moving forward in the best manner possible.

SELLING IS SERVING

I've listed a lot of challenges that you may face someday or even find yourself facing right now. The goal of this book is not to dwell on those challenges (spreading the negativity virus) but to show you the many ways you can rise above the crowd and not only survive today's challenges but thrive. As a true sales professional, what you do provides genuine, specific, and highly personalized service to people who have the need and ability to own your product or service. Selling is service.

As an individual or as an organization, you may face incredible pressure to put your product or service, your monthly quota, your company, or even your own personal goals ahead of the needs of your client. That, my friend, is the road to tragedy, not to achievement.

Clients are becoming more sophisticated in their knowledge of products and services, and in the new technologies that continually spring onto the market. More than that, customer needs are continually shifting with changes in demographics, economies (local, regional, national, and global), politics, and technology.

The winners in the future will be those individuals and organizations who take on these multifaceted challenges and turn them into opportunities to build strong and long-lasting relationships with individual clients.

That, my friend, takes selling.

In the following chapters I'll show you how to sell right now no matter what challenges you're facing. By that I don't mean "pitch" or "deal" or "handle" your prospective and existing clients; I mean provide genuine customer service designed to meet individual needs. I'll show you the steps I've learned from real-world, on-the-street, and in-the-trenches experience . . . the essential steps to *Selling in Tough Times*. But first, let's talk about commitment.

THE SELLING CAREER COMMITMENT

A selling career, like a marriage, is a commitment. As with any long-term commitment we agree to take the good with the bad. Of course, when we make the commitment, we're usually on the good side of things. We have strong hopes for success, satisfaction, and financial reward. We're excited about a new beginning and what the future holds.

Commitments are made to companies to represent their products. Educational commitments are made—to gain industry knowledge and to develop effective selling skills.

Time commitments are made to work the hours clients are available.

We even make commitments to ourselves and to our loved ones that we'll be able to provide a better lifestyle for everyone involved. Often part of the commitment is never to go back to whatever it was we were doing before—a job we hated for one reason or another. That's an important point, because sometimes changes we make to *get away from* something we don't like can be more powerful than those we make to move toward something new.

Usually, we get into a particular field or industry because it ignites a spark in us. We're enthusiastic about what the product or service does for those who use it and the potential for new developments and growth within the product line, as well as the potential financial rewards.

Think back to when you made your decision to represent the product you now help people get involved with. Do you remember your excitement? You were excited about the product, about the benefits it provides clients, the size of the market, and your potential for growth in the industry. Perhaps you met others already established in the field who were living the life you desired. Since thoughts create feelings, you should now be feeling that same powerful pull toward achieving success in your industry that you did when you first got involved. Isn't it grand?

My teachings are founded on the basics of selling. And, going back to your original thoughts and feelings about your current field is critical to the success of what you'll read in the rest of this book. We are going to reignite your fire and determination to succeed. You may be currently facing challenges of one sort or another, but unless your industry as a whole is disintegrating there's hope that you'll come out on top as one of the professionals who survives and thrives whatever today's challenge might be.

As with anything new, there's a learning curve. With the refocusing and review we'll be doing in this book, there's also a learning curve, but it should be a much shorter one than if you were new to selling because of the level of experience you already have.

One of the greatest aspects of a career in selling is that it's challenging. Too many people in the world go to work every day to face the same situations, the same people, the same type of work, and the same pay scale. In selling, there are countless opportunities to face new situations, meet new people, market new products, and earn great rewards. As with anything that offers high rewards, it also makes high demands of us. We have to put ourselves out there each and every day with smiles on our faces. We must constantly meet new people and be good at thinking on our feet.

As a salesperson you enjoy advantages and perks people in accounting or manufacturing never see. For starters, you probably have the opportunity to make more money than they do. You might drive a company car or have the company provide your laptop and mobile phone, and pay travel expenses. Unless you work in retail, you may not even have to punch a time clock. Your time commitment may be more flexible than the other employees in your company because you may need to be accessible to clients during nonoffice hours.

Even though I, personally, think selling is the greatest profession in the world and have made it my lifelong career (even today selling ideas to readers), all those wonderful perks must be tempered with some reality. Reality in the world of selling is that business operates in cycles. It's not unlike the seasons or the lives of human beings and even plant life. We all go through cycles of growth, maturity, and rest.

As the title of this book says, there are bound to be tough times. There may be lean times and even downright miserable times when your industry as a whole takes a hit. Maybe your tough times are happening right now and that's why you're reading this book. The best news about that is things will get better. On the other hand, if you're on a high cycle and wondering how to prepare for a not-so-high trend coming your way, read on.

The biggest challenge most people face when they don't work with an understanding of the cycles is that they're never well enough prepared today for what will likely happen tomorrow. In good times, there is so much business that they become workaholics or take on unprecedented personal debt, anticipating that those big checks they're earning will continue to come in over the next five, ten or thirty years.

When business is up and sales are easy, it's also easy to get lazy—to get away from sound selling fundamentals. It's easy to stop doing some of the basics that make for a solid, long-term career. Then, when the cycle spins downward, both your career and personal life can take a hit. That debt you took on during high times is now strangling you and making you work harder on making ends meet than you do on your job.

It's important that you set realistic expectations for yourself when you are dedicated to selling as a full-time, long-term career. It's sad but true that many salespeople stick with selling the same product year in and year out because it's what they know. It's comfortable to them. They wouldn't consider making any kind of change unless their industry simply disappeared . . . like the market for buggy whips did when the automobile industry exploded.

Rather than waiting for change to be forced upon you, whether it's due to the overall economy, your industry, or your geographical area, you need to make one more of those commitments we talked about earlier. You need to commit to improving your skills, knowledge, and contacts as the years pass. Far too many salespeople who stay average simply repeat their first year's selling experience every year until they retire. Doing this means that your income will rarely increase faster than the rate of inflation. Is that what you want? I doubt it.

When times get tough do yourself a favor and don't react . . . *respond* instead. What's the difference? A reaction is action taken toward or against something that impacts us. It can be instantaneous, practically done without thinking or by reflex. In order to *respond* to something, you have to take two very specific actions: (1) Stop, and (2) Think.

Hopefully, you'll use this book as a tool to help you do just that. When you feel like things are getting out of control, step back and take a serious look at what's going on.

You will not be able to fix whatever has gone wrong until you figure out exactly what is wrong.

Once you do get a handle on what is happening, you'll have some choices to make. Do you stay in the industry and ride out the current challenge? Do you change jobs and go with a competing company that's faring better? Do you leave sales altogether and come back to it when things improve? Do you start your own business without all the overhead of your current employer? Do you go back to school and educate yourself for another career? This can be a tough call—even tougher if you have been riding along on a nice wave of productivity and not preparing yourself for the potential "for worse" part of your commitment to your sales career.

STEELING YOURSELF FOR SURVIVAL

In order to survive any challenge that negatively impacts your selling career, you need to follow the Boy Scout motto of being prepared. So how do you prepare yourself for some unknown event that may pop up on the horizon?

You begin with a commitment to personal growth. Personal growth is a process of increasing your knowledge and effectiveness so you can serve more, earn more, and contribute more to the betterment of yourself, your family, and all of humankind. It demands an investment of time, effort, and money. Keep in mind that if you're not moving ahead, you're falling behind.

Surround yourself with winners. Find other like-minded individuals and feed each other strategies for selling in these times, positive news, creative ideas, and business referrals. Be careful not to involve anyone in this process who doesn't contribute. And don't you be the one wanting the gain but not giving your own positive input to the others.

To keep yourself moving ahead, I recommend that you allocate 5 percent of your time to personal improvement. If you work a forty-hour week that's two hours each week. It needn't be a two-hour block of time, although many of my students find that extremely helpful. You could commit to half an hour each day. (Go ahead and do the math. It does add up to a little more than two hours a week that way, but you do want to achieve long-term greatness, don't you?)

What do you work on? That depends on you. Rate your skill level in the following areas that are critical to overall success:

- Time management
- Computer skills
- Writing, composition
- Focus
- Self-discipline
- Verbal communication skills
- Dress and grooming
- Business etiquette
- Body language—reading and relaying
- Reading skills
- Math
- Product knowledge
- Paperwork/entry knowledge

- Networking
- Prospecting
- Handling your personal finances

If you find yourself getting nervous about your current level of expertise in any of these areas, don't worry. The purpose of investing 5 percent of your time to improving yourself is to waylay those fears through education.

This educational experience need not be expensive or traditional (in case you're like me and hated school). Many resources can be found at your local library. Forget the ads for credit cards—a library card is the single most powerful card you can carry in your wallet or purse.

Can there be any better investment than in your own personal growth? Think about it. I believe you'll agree that anything else you might invest in can lose market value, be stolen, or seized for taxes. On the other hand, the time you invest in bettering yourself will remain with you for life, contributing throughout your career to your self-confidence and your ability to defeat whatever life sends against you.

As an addition to the immense volume of educational materials available at your local library, I recommend that you create an educational fund for yourself. Set aside 5 percent of your net earnings into a savings account for education. Then, when an opportunity for education above and beyond what you can find for free comes along, you'll never have to say, "I can't afford it." You want to be able to take advantage of courses at your local community college or university. Some private technical schools offer excellent programs, for a fee, that can help your career immensely. Just like concerts, many excellent teachers bring seminars to your local area on topics specific to your industry or field. Watch for them. Schedule them into your calendar. Go and learn!

Psychotherapist Alan Loy McGinnis addresses this well. He said, *"All of us have weaknesses. The trick is to determine which ones are improvable, then get to work on those and forget about the rest."*

In analyzing your strengths and weaknesses in the categories listed above, there are bound to be some things that you find easier than others. Those that you find difficult or uncomfortable will likely make the biggest difference in your career once you educate yourself on them. Initially, you may feel some hesitation to begin work on these areas. That's quite normal. We hesitate to do that which we fear most. And fear is nothing more than a lack of knowledge.

My personal mentor as a young salesperson was the great sales trainer J. Douglas Edwards. Like 95 percent of the people in the world, I had a tremendous fear of public speaking. When Mr. Edwards learned that I had been asked to speak at a sales conference about how I achieved high levels of success in my field, he told me, *"Tom, if you will do what you fear most you will conquer fear."* Hard as it was to accept, I knew he was right. I accepted that offer to speak, then immersed myself in learning how to prepare and deliver a good speech. I will admit that I didn't do very well my first time out, but I did it. And the doing gave me confidence to do it again . . . as well as the desire to improve.

Explore every route that takes you higher than you are today. Don't shrink from what you fear most. Don't fear admitting your weaknesses. Exalt your strengths in your mind and you'll gain confidence for conquering those weaknesses.

YOUR ETHICS WHEN TIMES ARE TOUGH

When you are facing a challenge that could very well negatively impact your income it can create a high degree of fear. Fear is quite common when tough times are upon us. We fear a loss of security. This could include income or even our jobs. We might fear failure—or the appearance of having failed. Those are two of the biggest causes of anxiety in people facing major challenges in business.

When we're operating from a state of fear, we don't always think rationally. Irrational thinking and anxiety can cause us to do things we later regret. We may start telling little white lies to our clients, coworkers, or family members. We may take actions that are outside of our normal manner of operating such as omitting important information that might stall a sale. Or selling something to someone who doesn't really need it. In other words, doing whatever it takes to make the sale whether or not it's good for the client. Unfortunately, those actions can cause even more challenges than those we originally faced.

Please don't do that. Don't accelerate the downward spiral you may find yourself in by taking the low road. Even though it may temporarily relieve some of the stress and pain you're feeling, it'll never provide long-term satisfaction. In fact, it may eat at you for the rest of your life. Or it may start a bad pattern for the future.

When having to make choices under stress, we need a strong conscience to fall back on. If you're someone who has made a habit of telling white lies or rationalizing taking shortcuts in your presentations, you'll find your "wise decision-making" muscles weak and will tend to make bad choices. Rationalizing poor choices is lying to yourself—and if that's your foundation, you'll lie to anyone.

My teachings on the subject of ethics are quite simple:

1. Follow the Golden Rule of treating others as you would want them to treat you. Would I want to be forewarned about potential changes in the community that might negatively impact the value of my home? Yes. Would I want to be told that I should invest in a product now that I don't use regularly because inventories are running short? Maybe—if I truly needed or wanted the product. Would I want to be told this is the most economical investment for the product if it wasn't? Definitely not.

2. Set your own personal moral compass and evaluate everything you say and do in business and in life by that compass. For some of my students, it's an external thing. When confronted with a dilemma they ask themselves, "Would I be proud to have Mom and Dad know that I did this?" Or, "How would I feel if my kids knew this is how I behaved or handled a situation?" For others, it's broader: "What would happen to me, my career, or my loved ones if my acting on this decision was put on the local or national news?"

Many people hold their compasses within. "How will I feel after doing this or that?" "Will I later regret this decision or action?" "What is the reason behind my desire to do this?" If the reason behind it is anything other than helping others make decisions that are truly good for them or providing a much-needed service to your fellow human being (or company), you may want to consider an alternative plan.

Don't bring the emotion of guilt upon yourself. If something you're considering doing or saying will cause you to feel guilty later on, just don't do it. Guilt is a wasted emotion. You and you alone control how or if it even affects your life.

3. Be honest. If you're always honest, if you never lie to clients, you won't ever have to worry about covering your tracks. Even Mark Twain spoke of this. He said, *"If you tell the truth you don't have to remember anything."*

Psychologists and psychiatrists will tell you that much of the mental anguish faced by people who consult with them is relieved when people learn to be honest about their wrongs and then forgive themselves. Carrying the burden of dishonesty weighs so heavily on you. It affects both your mind and your body.

Part of being human is being fallible. We all make mistakes. Just make a habit of owning up to them, honestly, asking for forgiveness from anyone you hurt along the way, and then forgiving yourself. You'll walk with a lighter step and find more overall goodness coming into your life.

Never, ever, put your need or desire to make money before your commitment to serve the needs of others. That's the foundation of a truly successful and extremely rewarding long-term career in selling.

SUMMARY

- You understand that selling is a cyclical business and that you need to enjoy the highs, while preparing for the lows.
- Most of what causes changes in the cycles is not something you can control. You must respond to change rather than react to it.
- Selling is a career of providing service to others.
- A true professional makes a commitment to success in a sales career.
- In order to succeed, you need to hold yourself to your own ethical compass.

2. What Kind of Salesperson Are You?

Since you're reading this book, I assume you're not the kind of salesperson who glad-hands potential clients or pushes them into making buying decisions they may later regret. But our goal in this chapter is not to talk about what not to be. Rather, our goal is to show you the characteristics of today's top sales pros. Once you learn to recognize the traits of the pros, you can evaluate whether or not you have those same strengths, and if not, what you can do to develop them.

You have to work harder on yourself than you do on your job if you want to achieve true success. Make selling your hobby as well as your career. Develop the habit as you go about your day to watch all the various interactions you see others engaged in. Everyone is selling something! How are they doing it? What's their demeanor? What words do they use? How is the potential client responding to their style of delivery? Are they asking questions, spouting information, or giving orders? Are they succeeding? How might they have said or done something differently in order to succeed?

Keep your mental antennae tuned in to how every encounter you have provides you with ideas for better selling, and you'll soon find yourself improving daily. It can be something you say practically without thinking that gets your child to choose a healthy breakfast. Perhaps you hear your spouse say something to another family member that triggers a positive response. How did they get that response?

If you listen to the radio on your way to work (instead of listening to educational CDs), pay close attention to how each ad spot makes you feel. What words are being used? What emotions are being evoked? If you decide to write down a Web address or phone number from one of those ads, think about why. Was it because you truly need that service? Or was there something in the ad that appealed to you emotionally, logically, or rationally?

Many of my most successful students keep a notebook with them at all times to jot down little tidbits of selling strategy they encounter as they go about their days. Then, once a week, they read through them and think about how to incorporate those ideas into their selling situations. Try it! You should find yourself pleasantly surprised with what it brings you.

YOUR SELLING STYLE

Now that you're prepared to look for selling ideas everywhere you go, let's take a look at how you are selling right now. Most people in the world of selling fall into one of two very general categories when it comes to selling style:

1. The interesting extrovert
2. The interested introvert

Interesting extroverts are what come to mind when most consumers think of salespeople. Extroverts are people who direct their attention outside themselves. They are comfortable being the life of the party and always have a hand ready to reach out to someone new. At the extreme, these are the people who are often referred to as being larger than life.

At the more moderate end of the spectrum, interesting extroverts are warm and welcoming—always eager to make new acquaintances.

Someone who doesn't understand the more significant nuances of selling would tell the interesting extrovert that they have natural sales ability because of their "gift of gab," or ability to talk and talk and talk. In case you weren't aware of this by now, professional selling isn't all talk. When you are talking, you're only covering information that you already know. While it's important to have and share your product knowledge, it's even more critical to the sale to listen.

But what are you listening to? The voices of your potential clients as they answer your qualifying questions. Their answers help you determine what to tell them about your product—which features will serve their needs and provide the solution they're seeking. We'll go into greater depth about qualifying questions in chapter 7. For now, let's talk about the downside of being too much of an extrovert in sales.

Extreme interesting extroverts love to control conversations and hear themselves talk. While being in control of the selling situation is important, if you're an extrovert you'll need to be consciously aware of how much talking you're doing versus listening. Extroverts also tend to be so focused on what they're going to say next that they don't always stay focused on what the potential clients are saying now. If you have this habit, you'll miss a lot of the nuances and maybe some key information the client feels compelled to share with you. If they get the feeling you're not listening, they'll stop talking . . . and likely stop the sales process entirely.

Extroverts who want to be successful in sales need to lean more toward the conservative side of things and work toward a warm and welcoming selling style. Invite clients into your showroom or office. Make them feel comfortable and get them talking about their needs.

One more point about extroverts: they like being the star in their presentations and demonstrations. This will cost you so many sales your head will spin from wondering what happened. The star of every presentation should always be the product. The product is like a puppy up for adoption. You don't hold the puppy and talk about how great it is; you let the potential owner hold it, smell it, and get involved with it. While they do, stay out of the spotlight, and just watch and guide them to their decision.

Now let's talk about the other end of the spectrum—the interested introverts who go into sales. You may think that introverts wouldn't make good salespeople, but that's an old stereotype. In reality, introverts often do better than extroverts in sales. Yes, they may tend more toward an inner focus, but because of that they better understand the inner workings of the minds of potential clients. They tend to be more empathetic than the extroverts of the world, and empathy plays a key role in every selling situation.

Introverts may come across as somewhat humble or shy. In extreme cases, this trait would keep them from going into sales as a career. However, top sales professionals understand the power of having an attitude of servitude—of being a humble servant to the needs of their clients.

My dear friend and fellow trainer, Zig Ziglar, has always said, *"You can have anything you want in life if you'll just help enough other people get what they want."* That's the attitude of servitude I'm talking about—helping other people get what they want and need.

Another trait of successful introverts in selling is that they would rather listen than talk. They don't mind giving up control of the conversation. They let the clients talk and talk and talk—all the while gaining information they need to know in order to guide the clients to the right product or service. They serve as a filter, weeding out all extraneous information to select just the bits and pieces they need to help them determine which product or service will best serve the client's needs.

Consider where you would place yourself on a sliding scale with interesting extroverts on the far left and interested introverts on the far right. Which of their traits do you have? Which should you develop more intensely? How do you intend to practice these new skill sets?

If you're more the extrovert type, make a conscious effort to intently listen to the other person in the next conversation you have. Resist the urge to interject commentary into their story. If someone tells you about how their day went, listen and comment only on their day. Don't switch the conversation to how your day went or how you would have handled their situations differently. Doing this can be quite the challenge for the extreme extrovert, but the closer you can move toward center on the scale, the more your sales will increase.

For the introverts, it's in your best interest to work on making good eye contact with clients, smiling more, and using your body language to show that you're paying attention. Nod your head. Make a note. Lean forward as you intently listen. These body-language cues will keep your potential clients talking because you're drawing them out. Because of your level of interest, they will want to tell you more.

TRAITS OF THE TOP SALES PROS

Be more concerned with your character than your reputation because your character is what you really are, while your reputation is merely what others think you are.
      —John Wooden, former UCLA basketball coach

Now that we've covered your basic selling style, let's drill down into the traits and characteristics of the top sales pros.

1. Sales professionals are on a mission. Top people in every field are working for something beyond the financial rewards. They have something to prove to someone—even if that someone is themselves. Perhaps they were inspired by a success story of someone else. Or they have found a mentor who sees something more in them than they see in themselves. Some are motivated to succeed simply because they were once told they were average and that ignited a spark in them to be different, to be more, to do something unexpected that would set them apart as unique. Yet others are working for a greater cause and have found the profession of selling as a means to an end.

These top sales pros understand and appreciate the value in the saying I teach at the end of my sales training seminars. "I hereby commit to *learn more* so I will be able to *serve more*. Thus, I will *earn more* so I can build my financial net worth by *saving more*. Then, I will arrive as a Champion and be able to *give more*."

It doesn't matter if the "give more" part involves giving to immediate family or loved ones, or to give to the greater good of humanity or to saving the planet. Having a sense of purpose is what keeps you going when the going gets tough, as it's bound to do in this challenging yet oh-so-rewarding career of sales.

What's motivating you? What makes you get out of bed every morning and do what you do? If the answer is "providing for my family," that's fine. However, since we're internally motivated beings, what do you get out of providing for your family? Is it a sense of honor and accomplishment? Do you truly enjoy what you do? Or does it just pay the bills? Do you find serving others rewarding above and beyond the financial aspects? Do you love what you sell?

If you didn't have many positive answers to those questions, you might want to consider changing the product or service that you represent. You already have decent selling skills and one of the best benefits of learning how to sell is that those skills are transferable.

It's amazing what happens when you are representing a product that you truly love and believe in. People buy from you based more on your own belief and conviction about the product than on your rote delivery of product information. If you don't believe that your product is something so wonderful that you own it yourself (or would if it were affordable to you) and would get your mom, dad, and grandma involved in it, it will show in your demeanor during presentations with potential clients. Something about your delivery will seem off to them. It may not be anything you say or even your voice inflection, but something more subtle. Savvy consumers will pick up on your vibe and may decide to shop around. They may not necessarily be shopping for a different product, but rather for a different salesperson—one who truly believes in the product and can get them excited about it as well.

2. Sales professionals are detail oriented. They pay fast attention to details and operate like a business. Being disorganized is a huge obstacle to sales. Take a moment now to look at your desk, your briefcase, how your files are set up on your computer. Are they well organized? Can you locate pertinent product information at the click of your mouse? Can you easily locate complete contact information on each and every client? Do you have organized files? Is your paperwork complete? Do you track your sales statistics or have someone you report to who does? Or are you a piler? Do you have stacks of industry magazines or new product brochures sitting around that you haven't gotten around to reviewing? Do you use a calendar for planning activities beyond meetings with clients and sales meetings?

If you are not well organized, start today to handle details as they should be handled. Don't get stuck procrastinating because going back through all your files is a daunting task. Just begin doing it correctly from this day forward. Then, put in your weekly calendar a twenty- to thirty-minute time slot for "organizing." During this time slot, update contact information for your clients, do your paperwork filing, and read at least one magazine article or piece of information about your industry or product.

Note: Do not do paperwork or any organizing activity during prime selling time. Schedule it for a time of day when your clients are not accessible to you.

Even though you may work for a company, you need to operate like a business unto yourself. Keep thinking, "Would I want to do business with me?" Anytime the answer isn't a firm yes, consider what improvements need to be made and schedule time to work on them.

It's rare that an established business can make major changes overnight. The same goes for you. But if you diligently work toward improving on a regularly scheduled basis, you'll soon find conducting business easier and more effective, and you'll find yourself doing more of it!

3. Sales professionals are extremely empathetic and focused on the potential client's needs. I find that too few salespeople truly understand the power of empathy. Defined, it's the capacity to understand another's feelings. It's the proverbial ability to walk a mile in someone else's shoes—but not necessarily to get their blisters. It differs from sympathy in that when you are sympathetic to someone else's situation, you are physically and emotionally affected in a like manner. With empathy, you remain who you are, in your natural emotional state. You have the ability to understand their fears, needs, and concerns without experiencing them yourself.

When you go through the steps to selling in an empathetic manner, you are able to help your potential clients envision how they can get from where they are to where they want to be because of your product or service. You're not an outside force trying to act upon them. Rather, you are seeing their challenges through their eyes and helping them to see your solution through those same eyes. You're helping them with the answer to everyone's naturally occurring, self-serving question of "What's in it for me?"

When I used to train primarily in the real estate industry, I would tell the agents to get themselves out of the way and to sell properties through the buyer's eyes. An example I'd use for demonstrating a property is to never walk into a room ahead of a potential buyer. The reasoning was that the buyer was interested in the home, not the agent. They should see the home as they would if they lived there, and unless the agent was planning to move in with them they shouldn't be the first thing the buyers see in every room. People should discover the features and benefits of a home through their own eyes—not through the eyes of a real estate agent saying things like "This is the dining room" and

"The master suite is fantastic." Perhaps the folks touring the home "see" the dining room as an office. They might not agree with you that the master is fantastic. Maybe they've seen something nicer.

If you work on developing your empathy and ability to see the situation through the buyer's eyes, you'll do a better (and faster) job of guiding them to the best solution for their needs, all the while having them say to themselves, "She gets it! She's totally tuned in to what I need."

To develop your sense of empathy start with your friends or loved ones. Think of situations when you've been able to see things from their perspective. If nothing comes to mind, then try putting yourself in their shoes about just one situation you know they currently find themselves in. Don't be judgmental. Just think about how they must be feeling, and consciously take the role of a disengaged third party. If you were an outside party considering their situation, understanding how they feel about it, what advice might you give? Be careful not to give advice unless it's solicited. But, know that in selling situations, potential clients are talking with you because of your reputation or job description as being an expert in your field. So with potential clients your knowledge is being solicited.

Selling is not about what you want to sell. It's about what they need to own. So you must be attentive to what they say and do, and to how they explain the situation that convinced them to talk with you. Understand their frustration about not having, being, or doing whatever your product or service will help them with.

Don't get in a rut with a rote demonstration or presentation of your offering. Listen to what their biggest frustration is. Show them how your product handles that need. Then go into other features and benefits in the order the client wants to hear them. Not only will this make your presentation better, it'll keep it more interesting to you if you change things up every now and then.

4. Sales professionals are goal oriented. They have written down who they want to be, and what they want to have and do in the next thirty, sixty, and ninety days. They have their annual sales goals set as well, and goals for where the family will enjoy their next vacation. They know what they want as their next vehicle. They know how many clients they want to serve this year and what date they plan to retire.

How do you achieve your goals? You break them down into manageable parts and pieces. Then you put them on your "to do" list and allow time for their fulfillment in your calendar. Once you understand that activity breeds productivity, you'll soon find yourself on your way to achieving all the goals you can think to set for yourself.

Here is a short list of activities you should be doing on a regular basis if you want to grow and succeed in sales:

- Identify new clients
- Cold-call leads for new business
- Arrange/confirm meetings
- Prepare presentations
- Give presentations
- Close sales
- Send thank-you notes

- Make follow-up calls
- Service accounts
- In-house paperwork/reporting
- Ask for referrals
- Receive referrals
- Send information (e-mail, postal mail, or fax)

These activities are not busywork. They're just the opposite. They're activities that generate business. If you're the kind of person who likes having a visual representation of how active you are, visit my Web site: http://www .tomhopkins.com/. On our Free Resources page, we offer a printout of an extremely low-tech Daily Activity Graph. Use it, and you'll soon find your busy-ness equaling plenty of new business.

5. Sales professionals have a follow-up plan and keep communication flowing. Each of your clients should receive communications from you at least six times a year. Are you doing that now? When was the last time you connected with each of your clients? If it has been longer than sixty days, you're falling behind. Set aside one morning or late afternoon in the next week to call existing clients. There's no need to sell them anything or feel like you're bothering them. Simply call and say, *"John, this is Bob Martin with Acme Products. I was thinking of you this morning and just wanted to check in to see if you're still happy with the level of service we're providing. If you have any questions or concerns about (your product/service), please tell me."* See how easy that is? You could deliver it live if the client answers the phone. If they don't answer, leave the same message on his voice mail but wrap it up with *"I can be reached at [your phone number] weekdays between nine and noon if you need to talk."*

When you have a long list of clients to contact, try making these calls in the early evening or at another time when you know their businesses are closed. If you work with consumers, call when you know they won't be at home. Your goal is to reach their voice mail or answering machine. You can leave your entire message without having to invest the time talking with each person just then. You can reach a lot of people in a relatively short time period and at the very least let them know you're reaching out to them. Then, when you can schedule more time in your calendar, make it a habit to arrange a longer visit either via phone or in person with each client.

Mix up the types of contact you make. Not every communication needs to be by phone. You can send an e-mail, put some information in an envelope and drop it in the mail, or even fax a friendly message to your clients. Consider using a service that publishes newsletters about your industry and send those periodically to each and every client. Let them know you care to stay in touch and continue to educate them about your product or industry with information that they might find beneficial.

Note: When sending e-mails, keep in mind that they may be forwarded. You know yourself how easy it is . . . one click . . . to send messages on to others. Don't send anything you would not want someone else to see!

One of the easiest things to do that helped build my business from nothing to being 98 percent by referral in three years was that I sent handwritten notes to my clients on a regular basis. In fact, one of my daily activity goals was to send ten thank-you notes each and every day. I thanked people I met for the first time just for the time we shared. I thanked past clients for their continuing business. I thanked the people I did business with for their outstanding service. I sent anniversary thank-yous, thank-yous for taking my call. I sent thank-yous for the opportunity to present my offering (even if they didn't buy).

You might think I was a bit of a fanatic about it, but the proof is in the results. It worked! When any of those people I sent notes to had a real estate question, my name came to mind and they called me. They had plenty of my business cards because I included one with every note.

Today you can automate these types of messages to your clients through an online service such as SendOutCards. It's much less time-consuming than what I was doing, but certainly just as effective. I've provided information about it on my Web site.

If you're not confident in your ability to write an effective thank-you note, the wording my students and I have used for years is given on my Web site. (See page 239 for the URL.)

6. Sales professionals handle challenges promptly. This includes returning calls as quickly as possible, researching the details of what caused the challenge and finding creative ideas for resolving them. No one wants to face an angry client. Yet delaying a response to their challenge will only create more challenges down the road. Don't feel that you have to have a solution before you contact them. Think about how you feel when you're unhappy with something. Isn't it better when someone just gets back to you quickly to either gather the details or just to listen to you vent? Once calmness and clarity reign, solutions can be sought and provided. The better you are at resolving the inevitable challenges associated with being in sales, the more your business will grow—by referral. You can bet John and Sally will be telling everyone they know about their challenge. Don't you think it's wise to give them a happy ending to the story?

Even if you are unable to resolve their challenge fully or immediately, stay in touch with unhappy clients until they're satisfied or ready to move forward—continuing to do business with you.

7. Sales professionals present themselves with calm, humble, and competent demeanors at all times. No one wants to buy from someone who's on an emotional, physical, or financial roller coaster. It doesn't matter if you're at the top of your game and earning more this week than you earned all of last month, or if you're at the bottom of your game and don't know where the next client will come from. No one outside of you, your immediate supervisor, and your loved ones should be able to tell there are any challenges in your life.

Unless they're extreme sympathetics, clients don't care what kind of day, week, or month you're having. Heck, in some cases in retail, they don't even care if they know your name.

All the same, every person on the planet is intuitive. They pick up on vibrations or nuances in every situation.

Some people are more aware of this than others. Some will just get a bad gut feeling about you, your product, or your company and not want to do business with you.

Your goal as a top pro in sales is to come across as positive, competent, and calm, reassuring your potential clients that they are wise to be talking with you . . . wise to be considering ownership of your product . . . and wise to be making a decision today no matter what is going on in your personal or business life.

When you think of "wisdom," doesn't it give you a quiet, calm sensation? That's what you want to instill in everyone you come in contact with—that they're wise to be taking care of this particular buying decision at this moment in time. You won't get there if you're preoccupied about the last phone call you had from your spouse or about the sales quota you're not reaching or about the next thing you have to do after meeting with these people.

Let's look to the medical field for a good example of this. If you have a good physician you'll get the impression that when you're with him that you're the most important patient in the world. You and he may both know that there's a waiting room full of people who need his knowledge, but for those few minutes you're in the room alone together, he's totally focused on you. He's calmly listening to your litany of symptoms. He may be nodding his head in understanding. He's likely to be making notes and asking questions. This makes you feel important.

He doesn't come across as being arrogant about his superior medical knowledge . . . rather, he seems to be a great advisor who is sincere about trying to make you feel better.

You don't start wondering if he's having a bad day or if his family life is stable or if his business is suffering. It never crosses your mind that he may have something else going on that impacts his judgment about your current illness. That's because he's a trained and competent professional.

That's what you should be doing with each and every client. When you make them feel important and help them make wise decisions, they'll want to help you in return, hopefully by giving you referral business and, even better, buying from you again.

Note: If something comes up during your presentation that you don't know the answer to, don't just skip over it or make something up (a strong tendency in stereotypical salespeople). Tell your clients that you want to "verify that information" for them. Then, call your manager or another salesperson and confirm the answer. Demonstrating a desire to be accurate goes a long way to establishing your competency with clients.

HOW'S YOUR EGO?

Once you begin to achieve success in your sales position, others will start to take notice of you. Of course, you'll receive recognition from your sales manager for a job well done. However, you could also catch the attention of upper management. Egowise, it's pretty terrific when busy executives with impressive titles start talking to you about how fantastic you're doing. Your fellow salespeople will be watching you as well. How will you respond to all of this new attention?

There are four basic ways salespeople respond to new levels of achievement and its attendant notoriety. Some salespeople are basically humble people who won't like being showered with attention. They'll say little or nothing when congratulated and wish as hard as they can that they could turn into wallpaper and no longer be noticed.

It's okay to be modest, but your future successes will depend on how you learn to handle today's success. So you're out of your comfort zone accepting praise and recognition. If it's your desire to stay in sales and do well in it, you have to learn to handle the praise and recognition that comes with the territory. It's great to be humble, but not so humble that you don't allow yourself to accept the well-deserved praise of others and acknowledge to yourself that you've earned it. Let the effect of this new achievement take its course and increase your level of self-confidence. After all, self-confidence increases competence, and competence increases sales.

Force yourself, if you have to, to step forward and accept the recognition with grace. Take a lesson from others you've seen accept recognition and awards, even if it's from the Academy Awards.

We've all seen actors and actresses, directors, and writers get up onstage in front of millions of people and make complete fools of themselves. You don't want to do that, do you? Of course not. So, watch carefully those whose acceptances make you feel good and make you respect them. Study them and learn to do it with their style. Use their words if you have to. One word of caution, though: don't try to use the words of someone else in your company. Be more creative than that, even if you borrow your words from someone outside the company.

Another type of salesperson will accept the recognition earned by an achievement, but will downplay it by saying, "It could have been better." Or, "I could have beaten that record if only . . ." These people are so driven to achieve a level down the road that they never allow themselves to be happy with the present moment of glory. If you're one of those people, I say to you, "Stop and smell the roses." If you can't take a moment to sit back and bask in the exhilaration of achieving some great sales feat, you'll drive yourself into an early grave with stress and eventual burnout. For now, please realize that if you're always looking to some point in the future to be happy, you'll be missing a lot of great things that are happening all around you today.

It's great to have goals, and I highly recommend that you have your next level of goals in mind, if they're not already set, before you reach your current level. But never forget to allow yourself time to accept and enjoy the rewards of each goal you achieve. If there's no time for enjoyment, why strive so hard for the goal?

A third type of salesperson is one I hope you never become because it leads only to unhappiness and ruin. That's the salesperson who becomes an egomaniac when they receive the lauds and praise that come with achievement. If you begin thinking of yourself as a sales wizard and the hottest shot your company has ever seen, do you think the praise will last long? Probably not. It's okay to pat yourself on the back for making a tough sale or winning a contest, but don't take too long to get back to reality. You see, if you start to believe you're so good at selling that you don't have to work at it anymore, pretty soon you'll find yourself not working at it anymore. You'll be looking for another position.

The fourth type of salesperson is the ideal. It's what I'd love to see you become. When you are a top producer, accept the honor with grace. Thank all the people in the company who have helped you achieve that status. Give credit where credit is due. Be willing to share your experiences. If a new strategy or technique worked with your product, be willing to demonstrate it to the rest of the sales team— when they ask.

If they don't ask and you try to give them your best stuff, many average salespeople will let their egos get in the way. They won't want to accept help because it will be admitting they're not as good as you. No one ever wants to admit they're less than anyone else so be careful how you offer assistance. You might want to share an idea in a casual manner. Don't try to establish the "Joe Champion School of Sales Techniques." Others on your team who are really serious about their selling careers will usually come to you one-on-one and ask for ideas or help anyway. Give them all the help you can without putting a big dent in the time you spend with clients. After all, you won't be able to stay on top if you don't get out there and serve your clients well.

Keep in mind that any recognition you earn in your sales career is a compliment you receive for serving the needs of others. The key word here is *serving*. I have taught for many years that in sales your income is a direct reflection of your ability to serve your clients. Never forget that. Don't let your ego get so blown out of proportion that it interferes with the level of service you give. I'm reminded of a message someone sent me to share with my students a few years back. It's called the Salesperson's Prayer. It goes like this: "Lord, protect me from my own ego."

You must always have, at the minimum, as much interest in your clients as you do in yourself. If your attitude gets too high and mighty for them, then pretty soon you're not going to have any clients. In order to keep your ego in check, always think of clients as the people you serve.

YOUR FAME AROUND THE OFFICE

If your sales are rising steeply, there's another point you need to consider: how will your coworkers handle all the attention you're getting? It's been said that friends can stand anything except your success. More than a thousand years ago, envy was identified as the fourth deadly sin. It's vicious—and almost universal. If your personal friends will have trouble handling your success, how will the gang at the office cope with it?

A lot of how they handle your success will depend on how you handle the success of others. Think about it for a moment. I know this sounds a lot like the Golden Rule, but if you treat others with admiration and respect for their successes, they'll likely treat you that way when you succeed.

If others are challenged by your level of success, how will it be expressed? Subtly, because they can't admit, even to themselves, that they don't like you just because you're doing better than they are. But you may feel their disapproval, their coldness, their jealousy.

Of course, the more mature members of your team will be the first to congratulate you and wish you continued success. However, it's unfortunate, but the working world isn't filled with mature, competent individuals. It takes all types of people to make up the world and only one type is ideal. The other less-than-ideal personalities have to be recognized and dealt with as well.

What can you do with the people who aren't happy about your success and recognition? The key is to rid yourself of the idea that you must have their approval. If you crave the approval of the people around you, you're doomed to their level of mediocrity. Unconsciously, you'll limit your sales efforts so as not to upset your coworkers, which means pointing your career in the same direction as theirs. For most of the salespeople in the world, that direction is not very high up the ladder of achievement.

You have to make a choice. Are you willing to sacrifice your future for a warmer "Hi" in the morning from your fellow salespeople? Probably not. The best way to handle those people is to remain as positive and friendly as you've always been. Don't react outwardly to any jibes or comments they make. Take it all with a smile. It'll kill 'em. Eventually, the sport of knocking the top producer will lose its interest, and they'll leave you alone.

If you are not the top producer, rather than join the negative people in the office in condemning the top people you should watch those high producers closely and learn from them so you can reach the heights they've attained.

HOW DO YOU HANDLE A SLUMP?

We've covered situations where you are unbelievably successful, and we hope with the knowledge you gain from us and other sources that is the case most of the time. Now, how about when the results you're getting are unbelievable in the opposite direction? How will you act then? The single best first step is to find a mirror. Look yourself in the eye and say, *"I'm having poor sales because I am not serving enough clients or I am not serving the clients I have well enough."*

For some salespeople, the hardest thing in the world to do is to admit that it all comes down to that face in the mirror. It's called accountability and can be an extremely humbling experience (especially if you're not already a humble, interested introvert).

If you're using the Daily Activity Graph mentioned earlier, or some other method to track your activity versus productivity, you'll see a slump coming long before it hits and be able to take action to prevent it or at least soften the blow. If a downturn hits your industry as a whole, it won't be a surprise to you if you have kept up on your reading. Again, you should be able to see the warning signs and take action that will be in the best interests of both your clients and your own career.

The biggest mistake you can make is to blame a sales slump entirely on a down market or on negative press or anything else. Why? Because when you blame someone or something outside yourself, you give yourself an excuse and let yourself off the hook for something only you can fix. It puts you in a negative place. You allow yourself to wallow in self-pity or become absorbed in what's wrong instead of working toward something positive, good, and right—a solution!

It can be an equally great mistake to blame yourself for your entire sales slump unless you're the only person in your company having one. Markets will fluctuate. Competitors will develop better products or newer technologies faster than yours. Consumers will not always be loyal to your brand.

If the market as a whole is down, it's time to get creative with your selling tactics. If the market is okay but your sales performance is down, it's time to go back to the fundamentals of selling and bring your skills up to a new level of service.

CHANGING YOUR TACTICS

When it's time to think and act creatively to get new business, or to earn more business from existing clients, it helps tremendously to remain positive. I'm not saying to put on rose-colored glasses and try to ignore the fact that you're facing a challenge. Instead, look for the positive side of everything. All things in nature have an equal and opposite—up/down, left/right, inside/outside, and so on. One can't exist without the other. So if you're seeing a lot of negatives around you, it only makes sense that there are positives as well.

If your large clients are now placing smaller orders or placing them less frequently, they're probably feeling the same pinch you are. Rather than worry about your next order from them, think about how you can help them do better. As a sales professional, you encounter more people in different companies in a single month than the average employee at a single company does in a year. Think about what Company A is doing to survive the current market challenge and consider if it's something Company B might also benefit from. Of course, never share information between competing companies, but when appropriate, be a walking reference guide for all of your clients. Not only will they thank you verbally for the input, they'll thank you with their continued business.

If you're not investing all of your time servicing your largest accounts because they've cut back, invest more time with your smaller accounts. They may appreciate the added attention, and you might find new avenues to sales through increased business with them or from referrals they hadn't given you before (when you weren't giving them your highest level of service).

Commit time in your weekly schedule to reach out to potential new clients (aka prospecting). You can do this by phone, mail, e-mail, or fax. Start with considering your existing client base. Who is your ideal client? What type of business? Or, do you primarily serve families? If it's families, are they mostly young—just starting to own property and have children? Or are they a bit older, with different needs?

Once you have clarity on the demographic of your ideal clients, seek out referrals to those folks or consider joining a social group (if appropriate) where you'll find them. If you don't already participate in networking opportunities, look for them right there in your town. You may be surprised to learn that a great group of people who will support you and send you referral business is already meeting right down the street once a month or even more frequently.

GOING BACK TO THE FUNDAMENTALS OF SELLING

If you and you alone are facing a sales slump, it's time for "spring training" or "preseason training camp." All professional athletes begin at the beginning before every season. In order to begin a new successful selling season, you need to do the same.

You don't necessarily have to go anywhere, but it might help to get away from your daily environment to refocus on the basics of selling. Think about when you were new to sales. What did you do each day? Probably not much compared to your activity when you were at the highest point of your career. However, the foundation laid then by gaining product knowledge, talking with others who were doing better than you, attending meetings and training classes, and making tons of calls to potential new clients set the stage for the growth that followed. Depending on how deep your slump is, you may not have to go back that far, but it's a good idea to review your activities back then and add some of them into today's schedule.

Look upon your sales slump as a rebuilding opportunity. The new skills you acquire and the resilient attitude you develop to overcome any slump will serve you well for the rest of your career.

SUMMARY

- You have made selling your hobby. Your antennae are up all the time for new ideas for selling successfully.
- You know your current selling style and are taking action to include the right mix of introvert and extrovert in your new and improved selling style.
- You are developing the traits of the top sales pros.
- Your ego is in check. You can handle both success and nonsuccess with equal grace and character.

3. What Stage of the Cycle Is Your Business in Now? (And What to Do About It)

Those who cannot remember the past are condemned to repeat it.

—George Santayana, Spanish philosopher

While I'm no economic genius, I can speak from my own experience based on several decades in business. Business the world over runs in cycles. The typical business cycle has many stages. The stages I have observed tend to follow this pattern.

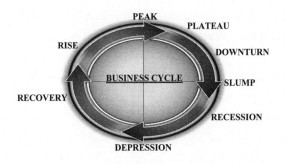

Within each stage, only three things can happen: (1) things improve, (2) things stay the same, (3) things get worse.

This is not rocket science. It's a cycle, a pattern, a season. There are seasons for business just as there are for our personal lives and in nature. As professionals dedicated to succeeding in both our business and personal lives, we need to grasp this and always follow the Boy Scout motto of being prepared. The longer we try to hang on to a cycle that's ending for whatever reason, the more difficult we'll find it to succeed in the next one. Typically the reason for hanging on to the past is that we're not prepared for the future. In some cases, we just weren't paying attention. That has to stop.

Let's go into more detail about these stages so you will continue to succeed throughout your selling career.

Being a generally positive person, I'll begin with the Peak. This is when business is good. The unemployment rate is low. Advancements are being made seemingly daily in technology and the medical world and worldwide trade is healthy.

One of the truest statements I've ever encountered is "This too shall pass." Whether you're happy or sad, whether business is good or bad, doesn't matter. This too shall pass. And if we don't grasp that concept and work within it, we won't be as successful as we could be otherwise.

As human beings we can only take so much new, new, new. It's been said that the typical human being needs seventy-two hours to absorb a new idea. Since hundreds, if not thousands, of new ideas and discoveries are literally at our fingertips each day, it only makes sense that eventually we will need to step back to absorb it all. That's when things tend to plateau.

Most Plateaus in my lifetime haven't lasted long, because as soon as folks recognize it something happens. Someone gets a new idea for marketing an old product or to reach a new market for that product. A great example for this is automobiles. Did you know that when automobiles were first mass-marketed they only came in one color? Black.

Here's an excerpt about that from the free online encyclopedia, Wikipedia:

Henry Ford is commonly reputed to have made the statement "Any customer can have a car painted any color that he wants so long as it is black." Actually, Model Ts in different colors were produced from 1908 to 1914, and then again from 1926 to 1927. It is often stated that Ford chose black because the paint dried faster than other colored paints available at the time, and a faster drying paint would allow him to build cars faster since he would not have to wait as long for the paint to dry.

Over thirty different types of black paint were used on various parts of the Model T. These were formulated to satisfy the different means of applying the paint to the various parts, and they had distinct drying times, depending on the part, the paint, and the method of drying. Ford engineering documents suggest black was chosen because it was cheap and durable.

Can you imagine where we'd be today if that philosophy had held? What if we all accepted "cheap and durable" as the standard for everything we owned? We would all be driving black cars and be dressed in natural fabrics and colors. The natural-fabric idea is probably a good one, but I doubt many fashion designers (or consumers, for that matter) would go for all natural colors.

If you know anyone who lived through the Great Depression of the 1930s, you may know they were the original recyclers because it was all they knew. Anything that wasn't cheap and durable was an extravagance. And more often than not you would find new uses for old things. Some of the lessons learned during those lean times have been brought forward in a valuable manner, but as the quote opening this chapter states, we are also repeating some mistakes from history.

Let things plateau long enough and people get itchy for change. In many cases, change comes as a welcome relief. People and businesses buy more, and this leads to a Rise in the market. However, some businesses make poor judgment calls in trying to scratch those itches and produce either shoddy products, too many products, or— due to poor market research—a product that few people want to own. In that case, the market becomes flush with supplies.

During the change, new jobs were created, equipment was invested in to produce the products, marketing dollars were committed, and distribution lines were put in place. When warehouses are full and there's not enough demand, those industries move into the next stage—Downturn.

What Stage of the Cycle Is Your Business in Now?

Success in life comes not from holding a good hand, but in playing a poor hand well.

—Denis Waitley

An economic downturn is your time to step back and take that seventy-two hours mentioned earlier to reevaluate your own position in the economy. How solid is your personal financial situation? Are you one of the good ones in your industry who will keep afloat if things turn worse? If not, what's your Plan B? Are you prepared to take on more business if things improve?

Remember, selling is service. If you aren't prepared to serve more clients as things get better, you may be the cause of your own downturn in business. If you don't have a list of cost-cutting measures you can put in place if things don't improve (see chapter 11), you could damage your potential for recovery.

The next stage is a Slump. Who in sales has never had one? Not many career salespeople, that's for sure. We talked a little about slumps in chapter 2, but let's really define it here. A slump is a sudden decline in productivity. Whether it's your own productivity or that of your company or industry doesn't matter. It will show up in your personal bottom line. To get out of a slump, there are things you can do personally and suggest to others in the company.

First, acknowledge that you're in a slump. This can be the hardest part. Denial is common when facing unpleasant developments, especially those that negatively affect our security (spelled M-O-N-E-Y). When sales are down sharply, admit that you're in a slump. Then resolve to take vigorous action that will allow you to work your way back into solid production.

Second, find out why you're slumping. If you've kept accurate records you'll quickly be able to see if the current slump is self-induced (not being as active as you once were) or caused by an outside force. Until you know precisely what has infected your sales performance, you won't be able to take the cure.

Third, plan how you will counteract your current slump. If you're in a personal slump and you see that you've gotten out of the habit of prospecting, that's where you pick things up. It may be time to investigate some alternative methods of prospecting, such as online or through networking groups. If your slump is because you're not staying in touch with current and past clients, that's an easy fix—though you may have to swallow your pride and admit to some of them that you've been lax in addressing their needs. If you provide a quality product at a fair market investment, most folks will forgive you and stick with you as long as you don't make a habit of ignoring them.

If the slump is caused by something outside the organization, start talking with others in the industry to learn more about what's happening. Take an in-depth look at what you are or are not doing to keep market share. Then look at what the competition is doing to achieve the same. It should become blatantly obvious what moves you need to make.

If everyone is suffering a downturn in productivity, you may need to get creative. Do some research on other industries that are holding their own or doing well. Are there ideas you can pick up from them that might apply to your business?

The fourth unslumping step is to take action. Don't invest so much of your time and effort in analysis that things drop off into the next stage (Recession) before you do something about the slump. Diligently pursue the information you need, but start pushing up out of the slump as quickly as possible.

The next phase of our business cycle is Recession. Defined, it is the contraction phase of the business cycle, a period of reduced economic activity.

Since the year 1919, there have been at least sixteen periods of recession, the average length of which was thirteen months. Never fear, even though we are covering a not-so-positive subject here; there have been over thirty cycles of expansion during that same time period.

Many of those recessions hit certain industries harder than others. In the 1970s, there was an oil crisis. There was a shortage of gasoline and folks had to wait in long lines to gas up their vehicles. Prices per gallon went up by 150 percent.

In the early 1980s high mortgage interest rates negatively impacted the real estate market and everything related to real estate. Also affected at that time were steel manufacturing and automobile production.

The early 1990s saw the collapse of the savings and loan industry. In the late 1990s many of us suffered through the dot-com mess.

In the early 2000s many people in the United States benefited from an economic bubble. The housing market was booming. It was easier than ever to get a mortgage. The jobless rate was low. People and businesses were consuming at a phenomenal rate. The stock market was reaching new highs. Happy days were truly here again!

Then, we blew that bubble up just a little too big for its own good, and it burst. The cycle started to change, the market began to rebalance and many people and businesses lost their footing.

The interesting thing that happened was a convergence of cycles. You see, the real estate industry runs roughly on an eighteen-year cycle. Other industries run twelve years. Yet others take ten years to run through a cycle. Some cycle through in as little as four years.

I'm no mathematician, but even I can see that several of these industries all hit the downward curve in their cycles very close together. Some industries were powerfully impacted by the politics of the time, while others simply ran their normal course. Add to that a U.S. presidential election with no incumbent, and we can talk about uncertainty until we're all blue in the face. My focus as a public speaker during times like that is to tell people to stop talking about all the negativity and do something positive.

> *Once a person* believes *that something is true (whether it is true or not), he then* acts *as if it were. He will instinctively seek to collect facts to support the belief no matter how false they may be.*
>
> —Robert Anthony

Recessions, no matter what size or length of duration, tend to create uncertainty and fear in the minds of consumers and businesses. However, you're reading this book today and know that there have been periods of growth and expansion to counter all those past recessions. Not unlike waking to the result of an overnight blizzard, eventually we dig ourselves out and get on with our lives.

Depression. In the early 1920s, the American economy was booming. We had emerged from The Great War (World War I) victorious and optimistic. Average Americans were busy buying automobiles and household appliances on credit, enjoying the Jazz Age and new freedoms. Many were speculating in the stock market as well. Our new habits and practices were unsustainable, though. In October 1929, the stock market crashed, triggering the worst economic collapse in the history of the modern industrialized world. It spread from the US to the rest of the world and lasted nearly twelve years! Banks failed. Businesses closed and more than 15 million Americans became unemployed. People were forced to develop habits of careful saving and frugality. Prior to the Great Depression governments traditionally took little or no action in times of business downturn relying on market forces to achieve the necessary economic corrections. This depression was just too deep to recover quickly so the governments intervened with regulations, public works, social-welfare services, and deficit spending in order to kick start a necessary economic recovery.

Let's move on to Recovery. Whether in personal or

our business lives, during a recovery we start to see a slowdown of bad news. Our paychecks are stabilizing. Some of our clients are ordering in larger quantities or more frequently. We may even be getting more requests to bid against the competition. However, this is where most people feel the need to take baby steps. It's not unlike recovering from a serious illness. We may be feeling better than before but aren't ready to run any marathons yet. It's wise during recovery to stay the course in a steady manner, providing exceptional service to existing clients before attempting to expand (or, depending on how you look at it, to spread yourself thin with a large volume of clients).

The next stage, of course, is everyone's favorite—the Rise. This is when confidence is strong and creativity abounds. Everyone gets busy, not just the champions. They've been busy all along!

WHAT TO DO WHEN JUST YOUR INDUSTRY TAKES A HIT

In the mid-1960s, the concept of real estate time-share was begun in Europe. It crossed the pond into the United States around 1969. By 1975 there were forty-five U.S. resorts with over ten thousand members. Those who were becoming educated on the concept, then investing in and using it, were very happy. However, certain marketing practices in the industry, combined with greed by both the consumer and the salespeople, caused things to turn nasty.

Consumers agreed to tour properties just to receive incentive gifts, never intending to make a purchase.

Some of the salespeople were very unprofessional and a bit aggressive in trying to make sales when they figured out which clients never intended to own. The industry received negative press and worse—word on the street among consumers became negative. The industry needed help to turn things around. Well, they did, and as of January 1, 2007, 4.4 million households owned one or more U.S. time-share weekly intervals. Much of the turnaround was related to the industry itself raising the bar for its sales teams. More and more professional training was provided, and the industry started monitoring its own best practices.

In the mortgage and real estate fields in the early years of this century, there was more business than the long-term career folks could handle. Many newbies got into those two professions—many to make the quick buck that was available. Unfortunately, they didn't have the skills and experience to justify the incomes they were earning.

In some cases I would have to believe that homeowners who later got into foreclosure trouble didn't truly understand what they were getting into. They may have been working with inexperienced real estate agents or mortgage brokers who didn't educate them well enough. Or, they may have had the misfortune of working with less-than-professional salespeople or companies that took advantage of them.

Granted, it's a buyer-beware world and those buyers should have sought out a solid education before putting their signatures on any paperwork, but there is a tremendous amount of personal responsibility that comes with a dedication to professionalism. The foundation of all truly successful people in the field of selling is that the product, service, or offer must truly be good for the client. That term *good* should also indicate that it's a wise move for consumers financially as well, with regard to the benefits it provides.

So what have we learned from those examples? That the more professional we are, the less of an effect an industry hit will make on us. When you're one of the good ones who is truly serving the needs of your clients and offering a quality product, you'll retain a great deal of client loyalty during challenging times.

Please note, even though you may have a high level of goodwill with your clients, you need to be proactive in contacting them whenever there's negative press about your company or your industry. It would be best to contact them in person, the next best is by phone, and the last would be via e-mail or letter. Your message should calm any fears or anxieties that the news may have created and to let clients know you're on top of things and still looking out for their best interests.

When you reach out to them before they contact you, it adds to their confidence in your abilities as an expert and your dedication to the field. Remind them of the number of years you've already been in the industry and that you intend to remain in it for the long haul. Your own personal commitment and enthusiasm will go a long way toward settling their fears and keeping them as clients.

WHAT TO DO WHEN FACING A CHALLENGING CYCLE

The first thing to do is to keep your attitude positive. I know this can be difficult, but not doing it doesn't help anything. Letting the negatives get to you is what average salespeople do. And you're not average!

When you're down you're more likely to find reasons not to do the important things that make money. Why? Because doing those things could also lead to rejection. When you're already feeling down, your threshold for handling rejection tends to be low as well. In other words, if you allow your spirits to sink, your sales performance will, too.

Nearly every office has at least one person you can talk with for five minutes and feel emotionally drained. Pay attention to how much time you're spending with that person and cut back. Steer clear of them entirely for a few days if at all possible. Your positive attitude is a precious asset— even more precious when you're facing challenges.

Work on getting everyone you can influence to be proactive about being positive. Get your family or roommates looking for good news to share. Post positive quotes or sayings around the house so you see them as you prepare for your business day. You may not be able to have a major influence on what happens outside your home, but you certainly can set the tone for what happens inside it.

Do whatever you can to lessen the chaos that early mornings can be with getting everyone out the door. That chaos drains your emotional energy as much as a sales rejection does. Don't risk starting your day on the negative side of things. Keeping a positive attitude is actually a time-saver.

When you allow yourself to get down in the dumps, it isn't just your enthusiasm that's affected; your effectiveness goes down, too.

We already discussed that you must respond instead of react to events beyond your control. But what is an appropriate response to a down cycle? You want to work on activities that help turn any fears or anxieties you might have into energy. You want to pursue challenging yet realistic goals. As Gerhard Gschwandtner, publisher of *Selling Power* magazine, says, *"The economy may empty our pockets, but it cannot empty our spirits."*

So, we're going to get busy! Over the years, I've noticed that successful people—those who lead companies, build estates, and fulfill their highest potentials—don't spend much more time working than many unsuccessful people do. The difference is that the successful people have the ability to get more productivity out of every hour invested.

How do they do it? Their method is amazingly simple. In fact, it's so simple that many people just won't believe it works and won't even give it a try. I've taught this method to hundreds of thousands of my students over the years. Many have told me that it works for them as well as it does for me. Yet they still don't want to believe how simple it is.

The whole idea centers on not trying to do too much. It's an established fact that the average person cannot successfully handle more than six or seven things in their minds at one time. But, we try to do it all the time—at least until we learn the simple method of writing them down. Don't leave me here because you think I'm just telling you to keep a "to do" list. This strategy goes deeper than that.

Keeping a short list means that you narrow down what's truly important to do each day. After all, today is all we have, right? And writing (or inputting) them helps you to summarize the details and envision the tasks already done.

Believe me, I've used this strategy for years, and it's helped me not only to be more productive but to lessen the amount of time I spend worrying. I will admit that I am a major worrier. It's something I've worked on for years and still do. But I have found that I worry a lot less about getting important things done than I used to. I know I won't forget them because they're written where I'll see them every day.

The next step of this simple strategy is to rank those six items in the order of their importance. Earl Nightingale was one of the most popular public speakers when I was starting my career in sales. I went to hear him speak on a number of occasions and owned several of his recordings. On his audio program *Lead the Field*, he talks about using this strategy himself. Once a friend commented to Mr. Nightingale how he never seemed rushed or anxious, that he must be a very well-organized person. Mr. Nightingale replied that anxiety is caused by having too many things on your mind; by using this same strategy, he kept only one thing in the forefront of his mind—the task at hand. The focus that he harnessed by using this simple strategy allowed him to achieve a level of greatness few ever aspire to. When he finished Task #1 for the day, he reviewed his list and began Task #2.

Another side benefit of using this simple strategy is that if you create your list at the end of each day, you'll sleep better. Your subconscious mind will work on preparing you for the tasks of the next day while you sleep. You'll soon find yourself waking not only refreshed from a good night's sleep but with great ideas for accomplishing the day's tasks in a better and more productive manner.

When you first begin using this strategy, you may find it difficult to narrow your tasks down to six. That's normal. After a week or so of practice, it will become second nature.

One word of caution: Don't assume this list will allow you to accomplish twelve hours of work in an eight-hour day. Know your limitations. The goal is to have a smooth-flowing, productive day, not a day crammed with so much activity that you have nothing left to give to your personal life.

So, what will you put on this list? First and foremost, write down any scheduled events. This includes meetings with clients, internal office meetings, or personal appointments such as with your doctor, dentist, spouse, or child. Then move to prospecting according to the suggestions provided earlier. Even during peak stages of business you should dedicate at least 5 percent of your day (twenty to twenty-five minutes) to prospecting. This includes reaching out to new people through the phone, mail, and e-mail, and asking existing clients for referrals.

Next, I strongly recommend that you write down an activity related to increasing your knowledge. Go deeper into your product knowledge. Read up on the latest industry news. Analyze today's trends with your clients' needs in mind. You may be surprised at what you come up with. What if you found one idea that caused the majority of your clients to do even 3 percent more business with you. How would that impact your personal bottom line?

Be certain to include some sort of activity in each day that benefits your physical health. If you're going to play at the top of your game, your body needs to be healthy. Why work hard to earn an incredible income if poor health will make you unable to enjoy it?

Those ideas should get you off to a good start. On days when you find yourself without meetings with clients (hopefully a rarity), try to arrange a breakfast, coffee, or lunch with someone else in your company who is doing better than you are and pick their brains. Or, invest some time learning about new prospecting methods on the Internet that are working for others. Today we have more knowledge accessible to us, literally at our fingertips, than at any other time in history.

SUMMARY

- You have learned to recognize the various stages of the business cycle and have determined which you find your business in now.
- You know what steps to take immediately when there's bad news about your industry.
- You have learned how to increase your focus, and thus your productivity, with proper planning.

4. Going Back to Basics: Where to Begin

In order to succeed, you must know *what you are doing, like* what you are doing, *and* believe *in what you are doing.*

—Will Rogers

I love that quote by Will Rogers. It has a beautiful simplicity, as many of his sayings did. It applies to anything in life that's important to us. But for now, let's apply it to your selling career.

How well do you know what you're doing? What you are doing is serving the needs of others. This may sound ridiculously elemental, but when faced with tough times, it's time to sharpen your skills. If you doubt me, think about what happens to all the professional athletes in the United States. Before they face new line-ups on opposing teams, they freshen up their skills. We have spring training for baseball players, preseason for NFL football teams, and training camps for college football players. Even professional athletes benefit from continued training—going back to basics before every season. The late, great football coach Vince Lombardi began every practice season with the simple line, "Men, this is a football." He would then take them through the most basic concepts of what the game was all about. Why? Because it worked!

Even though you may understand that your job is to serve the needs of others, you may have a sales manager or higher-up in the company who doesn't quite see it that way. They may tell you that your job is to move product. And yes, they're right, but you only move it to people and businesses who can really benefit from it, thus serving their needs.

To do anything to the contrary would work not toward your success but to the detriment of your career. You wouldn't have happy clients. You wouldn't receive referral business, and your company probably would soon help you make a career adjustment—to another company. So moving product to the right people is the key.

Now, let me ask you this question: "Do you like what you are doing?" If you dread getting out of bed every morning, look for excuses like busywork so as not to spend your time meeting potential clients, and have a morbid fear of rejection, you just may be in the wrong field. Or, if you'll give me the benefit of the doubt, you may not yet have been properly and completely trained in selling to realize the fun and satisfaction in it.

That's what I've dedicated my life to: helping professionals like you learn how to do this job well—the job of helping people acquire products and services that meet their needs. If you still don't like what you're doing after you've tried the strategies we're covering in this book, go ahead and move on to another career.

Next, you need to be able to say without a doubt that you believe in your product. Is working in this particular field what some would say is "right up your alley"?

As examples, people who love working with computers usually make good computer hardware and software salespeople; women tend to do better at selling cosmetics to other women than men do; slender, health-conscious folks make better health club salespeople than those who are not so slender.

Why did you choose your particular product or service? Or did it choose you? Part of the reason these people are good at what they do is because they enjoy the benefits of their products themselves. Or, at the very least, they are fascinated by the industry. You can see the excitement in their eyes when they get an opportunity to talk about their chosen fields. That's the way I felt about real estate even though I didn't own any when I first started my career.

Early in my selling career, I went into the field of residential real estate sales. There were few men under the age of thirty, and even fewer women, in that profession. In the 1960s real estate was considered a mature man's field. After all, it was about construction and investments, and in those days the men of the world were typically the driving forces in those areas.

Since I was quite young when I entered the field, I actually had a few potential clients ask if my dad was in when they came into the real estate office where I worked. I'm sure they were thinking, "What could this kid know about construction and real estate financial matters?"

> *If you are young relative to the others in your field, beef up your image. If you're married, keep a photo of yourself and your spouse in your office. It's even better if you have children so you can show their smiling faces, too.*
>
> *Any awards or diplomas you have should also be prominently displayed. Clients may not necessarily read them in detail, but seeing that you have them (the real things—no fakes) will enhance their confidence in your abilities.*
>
> *What we call vanity photos of you with famous people, or at the very least with the leaders of your company, are a good alternative as well.*

As it turned out, once I learned how to properly sell, I did quite well because I worked hard to understand what people needed to know when making decisions about home ownership. I loved helping people realize their dreams of owning homes and building memories for their families.

Some of the women I worked with at the time became top producers because they were homemakers themselves. They learned about the construction details to satisfy their male clients, but they also could speak emotionally to the wives and young families about what makes a house a home. After all, that's what we all really want, isn't it? Somewhere to go that's welcoming and hospitable? Somewhere we feel safe and secure?

Think about it: can you remember much about the construction of the home for which you have the fondest memories? Sure, you might remember a big picture window or a huge front porch, not because of their construction but because of what happened there . . . watching a beautiful snowfall, experiencing your first kiss.

Selling is a business of emotions. People want to believe that they make decisions rationally, logically—but in reality, they make them emotionally first. Then they defend those decisions with logic. They rationalize. This is true whether your product is a piece of manufacturing equipment, life insurance, clothing, or dessert at a restaurant.

The conversations people have in their heads might sound like this:

Emotional—I want to look good at the next corporate meeting . . . professional, successful, confident.

Rational—I need a new suit in order to do that. I should be able to get something that fits my budget.

Emotional—Oh, look at this one! The fabric is really nice. I'll try it on even though it costs more than I can spend.

Rational—I'll try on this cheaper one, too.

Emotional—I really like the more expensive suit. There's no doubt I look and feel so much better in it.

Rational—And this nicer fabric will probably wear better than the cheaper suit. It'll last longer. I'll get it.

You may not believe it, but the same type of rational/emotional conversation goes on in the minds of corporate execs making decisions about building new manufacturing plants. Emotionally, they want to look good in the eyes of the stockholders, the board, or whatever. Improving production and economizing for the company are part of their rationalization.

HOW MANY STEPS DO YOU USE WHEN SELLING?

When the economy is booming, you're likely to find clients clamoring for your product. They want it. You both know it, and you're likely to take some shortcuts in a professional selling cycle to get the job done and to quickly move on to the next client. In those times, most clients are okay with that.

In some areas, such as the financial or banking arenas, being the shortcut king or queen will likely cause people to think of you as opportunistic rather than career and service oriented. So you must do whatever is most appropriate for each client. It's always about what the client needs!

When times are lean, you need to be prepared to go through each step in the selling cycle in its proper order and expect your clients to be more hesitant about making buying decisions. They may want and need your product but are fearful of making any type of financial or time commitment. You reassure them about the decision by taking your time with them, helping them get comfortable with the idea of owning your product, covering all the bases and summarizing the benefits they'll enjoy.

In tough times, you may need to invest more time building rapport before people will open up, tell you their needs, and provide the information you require in order to qualify them. Or you may need to sharpen your skills on redirecting clients to a more economical product if they don't qualify for the product they were originally interested in. Sometimes your clients may take longer to make the final commitment, so your closing skills will need to be sharp. You need to know how to work with their procrastination, indecision, and fear.

All in all, you need to know how to effectively use all seven steps in a proper selling cycle to succeed in this business—no matter what's happening in the economy or your industry. The seven steps are: Prospecting, Original Contact, Qualification, Presentation, Addressing Concerns, Closing the Sale, and Getting Quality Introductions (also known as referrals). I cover each of these steps in great detail in my book *How to Master the Art of Selling.* In this book, we're covering just the aspects most commonly impacted by tough times.

WHY SHOULD SOMEONE PURCHASE FROM YOU?

Let's move on to the bottom line of why someone would purchase from you—no matter what kind of market you're in. Even if you are great at getting them emotionally involved in your offering and have excellent points for rationalizing the purchase, why should they invest with you instead of someone else with a similar product? What makes you different?

The bottom line to being successful in selling is to help people learn to like you, trust you, and want to listen to you. This is the foundation of all of my sales training.

Even if you have the hottest whizbang on the planet at the most economical investment ever heard of, if they don't like you and trust you, they won't listen. If they won't hear you out, they won't own.

WHAT MAKES YOU LIKABLE?

The single best resource for the answer to this question is Dale Carnegie's book *How to Win Friends and Influence People.* That book and the courses developed from it have made a powerful impact on millions of people since it was first published in 1936. It's still available today, and I strongly recommend that you read it if you haven't already.

The foundation of Dale Carnegie's message concerns effective communication and making others feel important. Fellow author and speaker John Maxwell says it like this, *"People don't care how much you know until they know how much you care."*

A lot of how you express your care and concern for the needs of your clients is nonverbal. It's about having the right grip in your handshake. It's about how much eye contact you make with them. Remember, the eyes are the windows to the soul. If you're not sincere about your desire to serve or about your belief in your product, it'll show.

It's important to take a moment to clear anything else that's on your mind before meeting with a client. Your client should never be able to tell by your demeanor that you have ten voice-mail messages to reply to, a child to pick up after school, and a meeting tonight with your financial advisor to see how your portfolio is doing. Focusing just on this client and their needs will allow you to read between the lines with them and speak with them appropriately . . . all things that make you more likable in their eyes. To put it even more directly, you're giving them your full attention.

Another thing to consider is how you carry yourself. Do you slouch or stand tall? Do you walk slowly or briskly? How do you transport your materials—are they piled in your arms or organized in a briefcase? People who stand tall, walk briskly, and are well organized are perceived as being competent and successful. Interestingly enough, they usually are. If you're wondering about how you appear to others, randomly ask a colleague, friend, or family member to be blatantly honest with you. Ask them if you appear competent and confident. Be open to their advice and consider making some changes if necessary.

Do you smile when you meet people? This may seem a little like kindergarten, but it's true that more people will like you if you're smiling than if you greet them with any other expression. For a few weeks, develop the habit of finding mirrors wherever you go. As you glance at yourself in those mirrors, pay attention to what you see. Do you see someone who is outwardly happy or someone who is worried and harried? Don't obsess over this, just pay attention and make some conscious changes when you realize they're needed.

Another aspect of likability is general friendliness. Think about how you behave when you're relaxed with good friends. You call them by name. You try to make them smile and feel comfortable when they're with you.

I strongly recommend that you use your clients' names in conversations. Since one of our early goals is to get them to like us, we need to operate as if we are with friends (but not too casually).

HOW DO YOU BUILD TRUST?

At the beginning of any new client relationship, they're not likely to trust you. Expect that. You may be one of the most trustworthy people on the planet. Your friends, business associates, and loved ones may be so trusting of you that they would literally put their lives in your hands, but the new people you are meeting in sales don't know that. In many cases, the first time potential clients hear your name is when you, a complete stranger, approach them about something that they perceive you want from them. They don't perceive a salesperson as someone wanting to give anything but rather to take—their money and their time, things most people hold near and dear.

Before you can expect anyone to pay much attention to what you have to offer, you must build their trust in you, your company, your brand, or even your industry. One of the best ways to begin this process is something called an intent statement. This practice is something I developed with Pat Leiby. He and I coauthored *Sell It Today, Sell It Now—Mastering the Art of the One Call Close.*

Pat trains primarily in the time-share industry, one where most times you have only one shot at building enough trust with a potential client to make a sale. The intent statement is a very powerful yet simple way to begin a foundation of trust.

The intent statement is like an agenda but a verbal one. It usually begins like this: "The purpose of our time together now is . . ." or "John and Mary, if you don't mind, let me explain how this type of presentation usually goes." It's where you tell them what you're going to tell them. In essence, you're giving your client a road map of what to expect in the next twenty, sixty, or ninety minutes, rather than asking them to let you lead them blindfolded through a maze.

Then, as you do just what you told them you would, they begin to trust you. They'll trust your word. They may even start to trust the information you are imparting to them.

To make the intent statement even more powerful, include in it the option for your client to say no. This is something they want and maybe have even decided before meeting with you, anyway. Saying it out loud to them works wonders at dissolving the mortar that's holding up the wall of sales resistance common in every selling situation.

In some cases, the option to say no will also work to draw their attention closer to what you're saying. It's as if you're taking the product or service away before they've even had the opportunity to learn what it's all about. This little strategy is effective both at putting people at ease and in building their curiosity to know more.

Here's a sample of an effective intent statement:

Mr. Combs, I appreciate the time we'll share today. Before we begin discussing your specific needs, let me cover just a couple of points. Our purpose for this meeting is to learn a little bit more about each other in order to determine if we at Tomco have a product that will serve the needs of your company.

I'd like to start by acquainting you with our company, its track record, and our business philosophy. Then, we'll review your specific needs so we don't waste time talking about something that has no bearing here today. After that, if we both agree it's appropriate, we'll review specific products and services that you might want to consider.

Now, Mr. Combs, I am a salesperson and it is my job to help companies like yours choose our products and services if they're right for them. However, I do not believe in using pressure of any kind. My experience has proven that our products aren't exactly right for everyone. They may or may not be right for you. Only you can make that decision. All I ask is that you keep an open mind, and at the end of our meeting tell me honestly if you think our products will serve your needs. That's fair enough, isn't it?

That intent statement takes just about one minute to deliver—with sincerity. Use my words or write your own, but add intent statements to the beginning of your next contact (and every contact thereafter) and you'll soon find yourself working not quite so hard to reduce sales resistance.

WHEN YOU FINALLY KNOW THEY'RE LISTENING, WHAT DO YOU SAY?

You begin by building credibility. I already mentioned that people don't just buy your product or service. They buy you as well. In fact, they have to buy you first. They have to believe that you're a stand-up guy or gal. After all, oftentimes you are going to be the point person for the company to provide any follow-up service the customer may need after the sale. If they don't like you now, why would they consider a long-term relationship with you?

Next, it's time to share some stories, letters, or information about some of your most satisfied clients. They should be about both you and the product. This is a gentle way for you to toot your own horn without seeming to brag. You're not the one saying how great you are . . . your happy clients do it for you.

Talk about your company history, why your brand is so well loved by your clients and the number of clients served. All these points build credibility. Delivering them in a professional manner also builds in their mind's eye a picture of you as being extremely competent.

It's very important for potential new clients to hear you say that you're proud to represent your company. This instills confidence and tells them that you plan to be around for the long haul.

Here's how you might do that: *"John, I could have gone to work for any of the five local distributors of widgets. I chose my company because of the quality of the product and their commitment to stand behind it. In my own*

80

research in this area, I found them to be the best, and I'm proud to represent them."

With that statement you've also just planted a seed in their minds that the competition might not be as good without directly saying anything negative about them. Never, never, never knock the competition. Salespeople who feel they have to tear someone else down in order to build up themselves or their companies will never be truly successful even in the best of times.

IT'S TIME TO GET THEM TALKING

Enough about you. The next step is to get your clients talking about themselves and their needs so you can both, hopefully, come to the conclusion that this is a win-win situation. This tends to be the weakest area for most salespeople who come to me for training. They just don't know how to get their potential clients talking—to talk enough about their wants and needs for the salesperson to present the right mix of products and options when that time comes.

Think back to our discussion about how people buy based on emotions, then defend their decisions with logic. Many salespeople put too much emphasis on the specifications of their products and expect clients to "speak specs," when most clients (unless you're in a scientific or manufacturing field) are more interested in the product's benefits, which are emotional. In order to be successful in communicating with clients, you need to speak both languages and be able to make the translation in your head.

You need not necessarily become bilingual in the sense that you can think and speak effectively in, say, English and Chinese, though that might not be a bad idea. The dual language I'm talking about here is that of your client and that of your company or industry.

Every industry has jargon that's native to it. It's very important for you to know it well. However, it's for use within the industry. If your clients are outside your industry but use your type of product, they won't be as fluent as you. They'll have their own industry lingo. And, if you do business with a certain type of client—doctors, for instance— you would be wise to learn some of their lingo. You can do this simply by perusing an industry magazine, the medical advancements section of a news magazine, or an association Web site. Such resources are typically filled with topical information you might use as a conversation starter. Your clients will recognize that you've taken the time to get to know them a little better and this will help build their confidence in you.

The primary way to get people talking is to ask them questions. And not just any questions, but information-gathering questions. Some clients may consider them too probing if they go into areas where they're not comfortable. If any of the information you need to gather might fall under the category of "personal" or "financial," it's wise to begin asking those questions with this phrase, *"Not to be personal, Ms. Mather, but there are some details about your medical history that I'll need to know in order to do a good job for you here today."* See what you've done? You've told her that you know the personal questions might make her uncomfortable to talk with you about but that it's for her own benefit to do so. It demonstrates sensitivity on your part and lessens her discomfort tremendously.

SUMMARIZE, SUMMARIZE

Once you have determined a client's needs to your satisfaction, you need to be certain they're satisfied they've told you everything. You do this by summarizing those needs. "Mr. & Mrs. Patterson, let me make certain I have a clear picture of your current situation. You have told me . . ."

As you state each point covered (especially those that "point" toward your product as a good match), watch their reactions. If you sense any disconnect from what you're saying to what they may have meant, ask for clarification on that point. "I'm not 100 percent certain I'm saying this correctly. Can you help me clarify that point?"

As you cover this list of their needs, a mental picture will begin to form in their minds of the ideal solution. If you have ever played the game Pictionary, it's the same idea. You have a clear picture of the best answer for them, but now you need to help them see the same image in their minds. Your goal is to describe that solution in such great detail through your product information in the presentation step that they come to the same conclusion you have.

You will summarize again after your presentation and before asking for the decision. This is a critical component to selling. This time your summarization draws the picture of all the benefits they'll receive (fulfilling the needs listed in your first summary).

Envision this summary as the grand finale of a fireworks performance. You've seen some great individual fireworks or small groups of displays, but when you see them all together at the end, it truly is a grand image that leaves a wonderful lasting impression on you. That's the purpose of your summary after presentation.

Since "Good morning, Mr. Jackson," you've been building toward your grand finale of benefits that fit his needs. Give it the attention and detail that it needs to help Mr. Jackson off the fence and into an ownership position.

If you've been following all these steps, in good markets and bad, good for you. If you realize you have been skipping something we've covered here, start working them back into your presentations.

WHEN YOU THINK THEY'RE READY TO GO AHEAD

Once you're pretty sure the client is ready to go ahead with the purchase, what do you do? Average salespeople jump right into asking for the order. In many cases it's the right move, but in others it's not. Once you've made a wrong move at this stage of the sales process, it's difficult to recover—to rebuild the client's emotions to a level where they're heading toward making a decision.

Rather than wonder if you're doing the right thing, it's wise to test where they stand on what they've heard. One of the most likely strategies to be overlooked by both new and veteran salespeople is the trial or test close. This is used before asking for the final decision. It's a question that allows you to test their feelings about the product before you ask for the sale. It helps you avoid the uncomfortable situation where you ask and they bring a new point into the mix, thus throwing off your momentum. A test question can be as simple as this: *"John, how are you feeling about all of this so far?"* Then you wait for his answer. It creates a wonderful opportunity for you to stop talking, take a breather and check to see if you've done the job you think you have.

If John's response is positive, it's time to ask for the order. If there's any hesitation, you may need to ask him to elaborate on how he's feeling. This helps relieve pressure and will likely open a new avenue for you to continue selling and try for a second close.

Some people will be totally involved in what you're saying and find themselves agreeing with nearly every point you make. Then they start to feel the pull to make a decision and get cold feet. It's all happening too fast for them. They need to slow down the pace. You need to be prepared to handle this with ease and grace. Asking them how they feel, or if they understand why your existing clients are so excited about your offering, is a great way to take their buying temperature.

The strategies we've covered here should help you to bring more clients to the point of closing. We'll talk more about specific closes that work well in challenging times in chapter 10.

SUMMARY

- You understand that selling is serving.
- You will always consider the emotional side of selling as well as the rational side.
- You will work on being likable.
- You realize that taking shortcuts in the selling process isn't for you.
- You are developing and incorporating intent statements in all of your presentations.
- You know what questions to ask to qualify clients most effectively.
- You will never again make a presentation without summarizing both their needs and your product's benefits.
- You understand the importance of using test or trial closes before asking for the sale.

5. Start by Keeping the Business You Have

Building loyalty in your client base is critical for ongoing success. One of the greatest benefits of having loyal clients is that you earn a sort of residual income. You need to stay in touch but not work as hard to keep selling them as you did to *first* sell them.

The foundation for loyalty includes the right products for each client, excellent service, and consistent follow-up. A variety of strategies for keeping in touch with clients and getting repeat business from them will be covered in this chapter.

> *You've got to give loyalty down, if you want loyalty up.*
> —Donald T. Regan

This quote was originally intended for leaders in business and politics, but I think it applies nicely to sales. Rather than down and up, in sales loyalty is received when it, and excellent service, are given. During challenging times, this involves giving clients the same level of service you always have, even if their dollar volume of business has dropped. It means reaching out to them when you see a change in their level of business to help them find ways to increase their business. It includes taking their calls—always—even when you're certain they're calling with a challenge or to cancel their accounts because they're facing tough times and have to make cutbacks.

If you have provided an exceptional level of service to your clients, there's a wonderful side benefit. During tough times you will likely be lower on their list of services to reduce or eliminate than another company that hasn't provided your level of extraordinary service. They'll have a harder time cutting something they truly enjoy and value.

Your goal with your clients is not only to retain their business long-term but to create scenarios where they purchase add-on products. Keeping a client relationship healthy is akin to earning residual income. You don't have to work as hard with them as you might to gain a new client. That doesn't mean you can ignore them, resting assured they won't go anywhere else. Nothing is that certain in the world.

The key to healthy relationships both personally and in business is to give them the attention they need and deserve. If you have any children in your life, hopefully, you've learned that kids typically spell the word *love* this way: T-I-M-E. They may hear you say "I love you" all day long, but they truly know you love them when you spend time with them. They feel the love when they see you in the audience at their school plays, when you're in the stands at their sporting events, and when you take them shopping or out to lunch rather than giving them some cash and sending them on their way.

Kids don't care how much money you earn or what type of car you drive (until they're teenagers and want to borrow it). Time spent together provides a sense of security about the relationship. It's a matter of knowing that if everyone else in the world betrays you, there's always someone to turn to—someone who is always in your corner.

If it's truly impossible for you to be physically present, the next best thing is to call. Your care and concern are easily heard in the tone of your voice. At the very least, receiving e-mails (especially those with pictures) and cards "just because" are fun ways to keep in touch.

Take the paragraphs above and change the image from your children to your clients. And maybe change *love* to *care about*. The functions you attend might be local sporting events, a Chamber of Commerce luncheon, or a client-company open house. The point is that your clients see that you cared enough to be where they are.

Of course, you need not take this to the point where it might be considered stalking, but running in similar circles as your clients puts you on their level, which builds trust and loyalty. They know you get it—that you understand or at least invest a lot of time trying to understand their world.

When it comes to making phone calls to clients, it's best if they are scheduled. When is the best time to schedule your next call? At the end of each call. It can be as easy as this: "*Barb, thank you for allowing me this time to catch up on how things are going at YourCo. I would love to touch base with you again in about a month. Shall I call on the twentieth at this same time, or would you prefer to talk at the end of the day?"*

The time frame for the calls depends on the type of business you do. If Barb orders from you weekly, it's probably wise to stay abreast of changes in her company on a monthly or at least a six-week basis. If her company orders monthly, a sixty- or ninety-day call might suffice. The idea is to stay in close enough contact so you won't be caught off guard by any drastic changes in Barb's business, or have her stolen away by a competitor who gives her the attention she desires (along with a competitive investment for the product).

Note: Before you ask to schedule your next call, always ask, *"Is there anything else I can do for you today?"* This should become so embedded in your subconscious mind that you catch yourself asking your children that same question before sending them off to bed at night and before you leave your spouse each morning. In most cases, clients won't have anything else on their minds, but they'll get the message that you aren't going anywhere until you know all the bases have been covered.

If your clients order directly from you, either in person or by phone, with each order ask a couple of quick questions about how they're faring during the current economic or industry challenges. If the company is on an auto-order system, or has online access to place orders, your scheduled calls are even more important. While it may be a huge convenience for people to place orders online or set up an auto-ship method, they're people and need human contact of some sort to know their business is appreciated.

Contact beyond the order-related type is important. As an example, I strongly advise the sending of Thanksgiving cards to clients, but if that's the only time you contact them during the year, they won't likely be on your client list next year. They'll be on someone else's list.

My business associate, the marketing guru Dan Kennedy, has this to say about staying in touch:

> *I don't believe in a poor economy as much as I believe in poor follow-up. In the past year, I've* not *heard from the salesman or dealer I bought my most recent automobile from, the real estate agent I bought properties from, the clothing stores and their salespeople in two different cities of residence I've patronized in the past, the restaurant I used to visit frequently but haven't been to in six months. But I have bought a car, real estate, clothes, and gone out to eat. And it's a safe bet a bunch of those business owners and salespeople guilty of zero or poor follow-up are poor-mouthing about the poor economy.*

If your clients are consumers versus businesses, I recommend a minimum of six contacts per year to build their loyalty. I covered this a bit in chapter 2 when we talked about the value of thank-you notes and the many reasons you should send them.

When you have earned the business of a new client, it's a great idea to find out how they like to be contacted. Many people prefer phone calls. Others prefer e-mail. Yet others would appreciate an in-person visit every now and then.

When you have news to share about a new product launch, feature, or just general news of interest to your clients, don't send it to everyone the same way. Share it with them in the manner they prefer. This may take a little more time if you can't just pop off an e-mail with all of your clients blind-copied, but it will be well worth it to serve them as they wish to be served.

Consider creating a single-page document about the news that can be attached to an e-mail, copied and included in a letter, faxed, or dropped off at a client's office. The document and information remain the same. The method of delivery is all that varies.

WHAT TO SEND

The simple answer to that question is: *something of value to the client.* Some examples of this would be industry information, advice, reminder notices, announcements, coupons, or gifts.

EXAMPLES:

- In tough times, financial advisors are wise to send out advice about how to handle money based on various stages of life, along with an offer to review each client's particular situation. If a new product has been released that involves less risk than the stock market, information about that might be included (or at least some curiosity-building copy about it should be sent).

- Real estate agents might send offers for free comparable market evaluations so folks have current and accurate information on the value of their property. Even if the answer isn't what they might like it to be, most clients will appreciate having their facts straight.

- Insurance agents might be wise to help some of their clients save money, even if it means lessening their coverage a little in order to keep their business—or, if they're in a high-risk situation, increasing their coverage to protect them from others who might try to take advantage of them.

- Service industries may offer one service at a reduced rate (or even free) once the client has completed three, five, or ten other services.

WHEN YOU HAVE SOMETHING NEW TO SHARE

If you are offering a new product or service, don't start phoning everyone to tell them about it. Rather, if making calls is appropriate, begin by asking if they're still satisfied with your product and service. Then say, *"As a satisfied client, we value your opinion. If we were to offer new services, would you be interested to know more?"* Do you hear how nice that is? If they say yes, follow up with a question about the service rather than a statement, *"We have found that many of our clients fail to change their furnace filters as often as recommended by the manufacturers. What would you think of a service where you receive new furnace filters delivered to your doorstep during the week you should be changing them?"* In essence, you've told them what the new service is but not like a stereotypical salesperson. You've asked their opinion. It's a much softer approach and works well with existing happy clients. You have created an opportunity for them to tell you if they'd want to own that service. If they do, sell it! If they don't, ask what type of service would interest them. You might just come up with an idea for a new profit center for your company!

Plumbers might offer to check the screens in all the faucets on the property while they're at a location for a service call. If this is appropriate, take yourself off the clock first. Then do it. It's something few people think to do unless or until there's a problem. It's a simple gesture on your part and shows you're willing to go the extra mile.

How else can you serve your clients? I recently read about a small drugstore that was doing more business than the local chain store. They added one simple service that increased their sales by a significant amount. They offered the same products as the big chains. They even had drive-through service for prescriptions. The difference was that they had one of their clerks accessible by walkie-talkie from the pharmacy department. Clients who picked up prescriptions at the drive-through window were asked if there was anything else they needed such as aspirin, cold medicine, heating pads, bandages, or other items.

Think about it. If you are feeling so ill that your doctor gave you an antibiotic or a painkiller, you may want some of these additional products but not quite feel up to walking inside to shop. When clients mention they have those other needs, the clerk is radioed. That person picks up a small basket and quickly brings those items to the pharmacy area for checkout. This idea was not rocket science, but it launched the store's revenues into a new realm. If the customer has too many items to fit through the service window, they simply drive around front, and the clerk meets them out in front and puts their bags in the car.

What other offers would your clients find of value either for purchase or for free?

GOING THE EXTRA MILE WITH SERVICE

If nothing else, start a database of quality services besides yours that you can refer your clients to. If you're a plumber, have the name and number of a good drywall company or painter at the ready. Real estate agents are typically good about building this type of list of handyman services, landscapers, pool cleaners, and so forth for those purchasing resale homes or fixer-upper properties.

We should all learn a lesson from the movie *Miracle on 34th Street.* The Macy's Santa tells a child they'll get a certain toy for Christmas. When the mother hears what Santa said she's upset because Macy's is out of the toy. Santa tells her that Macy's competitor, Gimbels, has it. At first the managers of Macy's want to fire Santa for sending their clients to the competition, but when they realize the goodwill Santa has generated and see the increase in loyalty from their customers, the story changes. Are you finding that your clients have needs you can't serve? If so, be the hero and help them find a quality source for those needs.

If you are in business for yourself, or you work with

a small company, you should be able to move quickly to adapt to the needs of your clients. Be creative, flexible, and reliable. They will see you as being a part of their team instead of an outside resource.

If a single industry—yours—is hit with some negative press, consider sending out positive press of your own about your company's longevity, your track record of service, and your commitment to stay the course. Maybe even include some strategies you're putting in place to ensure continued service to your clients.

Another idea is to send service reminders. The automotive industry and related services do pretty well with this one. Who hasn't received a postcard or an e-mail reminder about oil changes, tire rotations, or other such services? The same applies to the heating and air-conditioning business. How could you apply this to your business?

If your company is expanding by adding more customer service representatives, let your clients know. Introduce the new people by name (with photos of their smiling faces, if appropriate) and a line or two about their expertise or position. Clients like knowing whom to ask for and having a mental picture of those they talk with on the phone.

Gifts such as updated road atlases and calendars are commonplace in the insurance industry. Clients have come to expect them. Not only are they handy, they save the clients the expense of purchasing these for themselves. Think of something your clients would enjoy receiving from you. Then plan when and how you'll send it. Keeping your name in front of them in a positive manner on a regularly scheduled basis goes a long way to building loyalty, which in turn generates referral business.

Speaking of referral business, do you have a referral program in place? Many businesses offer credits in certain dollar values for each referred client who makes a purchase. Your loyal clients who send you new business could earn enough credits to really make a difference on their next purchase. Some people will be so motivated to earn $25, $50, or $100 in credits that they'll send you thousands of dollars in business. And if they have credits built up with you, why would they take their business elsewhere? That's the value of working to create loyal clients!

HOW TO APPROACH THE UNINTENTIONALLY NEGLECTED CLIENT

In a perfect world, we'd be so well organized and good about fulfilling our duties that we'd never neglect any of our clients. But we're human. Things happen. And we will find ourselves in positions where we haven't given our best service to a client or two. Hopefully, this doesn't happen often (or won't after you apply the strategies in this chapter). However, as we covered in an earlier chapter, accountability is the name of the game. You are compensated based on how satisfied your clients are. If you aren't happy with your compensation, chances are some of your clients aren't happy with your service.

As difficult as it may be to work up the courage for it, your best approach with a neglected client will be the same one used when you first gained their business. If it was an in-person meeting, you should do it eyeball-to-eyeball. If you first earned their business over the telephone, call them.

You can expect the ignored client to be anything from neutral to giving you the cold shoulder to being outright hostile about your lack of service. And you will deserve whatever they give you. However, once you decide the value of keeping their business is more important than a bit of being taken to task or having them threaten to leave you, it's not so hard to do.

The first step is to admit your lack of service to them. No excuses. *"Ms. Joplin, I know I haven't given you my finest service. I hope you will accept my sincere apologies and allow me to continue to assist you with your pest control service."* You may learn that they've already found another provider. If that has happened, you'll have to work hard to earn the right to their business once again.

If they really haven't minded being left to their own devices, they'll tell you and you move right into a discussion of what's been happening with them or their company— listening to cues as to how you can help them with products or just better service.

When a client gives you the cold shoulder and makes it difficult for you to regain their trust, you have to humble yourself and slowly work your way back into their good graces. Trust, once broken, is so hard to recover. But, it can be done if both parties are willing. You may need to start with a smaller-than-ever order. *"I realize you may not be happy with me right now. However, I'm hoping you'll consider placing just a small order with me now to allow me to provide you with the level of service you deserve."* By providing extra care and proper follow-up service, you should soon find yourself earning their full trust and business.

If any of your clients are angry because of your lack of service and are more than happy to tell you about it, look at the bright side. They're still talking to you—even if it's not with words you like to hear. Since you know you deserve it, let them vent. Eventually, they'll run out of steam and calm down. Get them talking about how they would like to have their needs served. Once you are onto a positive topic of how you'll work with them in the future, you may just find yourself keeping their business. If they truly enjoy your product or service, you may just need to apologize and promise to do better. It's best if you are specific about how you'll do that. *"I'll personally deliver your first order and help your staff check it in. Then, I'll follow up with both you and your point person about the effectiveness of the product. If you have any further challenges with it or with me, I want to know so I can rectify the situation immediately. After that, I'll be in touch on a monthly basis. In fact, why don't you just tell me when and how you'd like me to stay in touch? I'll add that to my calendar for follow-up right now."* Practice delivering this with sincerity. If this situation has occurred you had better be sincere about this. If you deliver it too quickly, it will come across as if you're worried or frightened about losing their business. You never want to operate from a position of fear.

If they're having challenges with your product that you've ignored, that's a different story. Ignore them long enough and they may just go away to the competition, but they'll damage your reputation (and possibly that of your company) along the way. Staying in touch on a regular basis should prevent this from happening.

It's easy to be loyal to someone when you're personally acquainted. Think about where you do business. Do you always go to a certain dry cleaner or grocery store? Is it just because they're convenient? Have you even done any comparison shopping to find out if there's a better business for your needs?

We are creatures of habit and don't often seek out change unless we're unhappy where we are. But how did you get there in the first place?

For example, I have frequented the same dry cleaner for years. In my daily travels around town, I probably pass three or four others that may have the same service and may even be more convenient for me, but I don't even give them a second glance. I'm loyal to my dry cleaner. Why? Their staff always greets me with a smile. Many have been there for years and know me by name. They do a good job, and my items are always ready on time. They've gone the extra mile for me on a few occasions when I needed a rush job or minor repair. It all boils down to this: they make me feel good about doing business with them. Do your clients say that about you? If so, congratulations! You're bound to be a success. If not, you have some work to do.

HUMAN CONTACT

Most of what we've covered so far is about your outgoing connections with clients. But what about their inbound calls to your company? What is being done to make them feel good about reaching out to you when they have a need that can't wait until your next visit? Call me old-fashioned, but I insist that we have a real person answer our main telephone line during business hours. We could have gone the way of so many other companies years back by automating this. Believe me, I do see the value in companies where there is an extremely high volume of calls going to a voice-tree system, but I don't believe in it for smaller businesses. I believe the investment in having a quality receptionist as the first contact anyone has with my firm far outweighs that person's salary.

I don't understand how some companies expect to build client loyalty when the only incoming contact a client can make is with a prerecorded voice instructing them in how to get the answers they need. How many branches of the voice tree do people have to climb to get answers? If a client of yours has a quick question, what kind of hoops must they go through to get it? Do you direct them to a FAQ page on your site? While I understand the point of those pages is to answer the most frequently asked questions of your company, why put the obligation on the client to find the answer? What if the question answered on your list isn't worded the way they would choose? Why should they have to search at all when you have a modern convenience called a telephone?

While much of today's technology is wonderful, I fear that some businesses get caught up in the time-saving features without analyzing the potential for loss of business because they come across as being impersonal. Why would I want to spend ten minutes or more looking for an answer on your Web site that any one of your staff members should be able to answer immediately? How loyal am I to that voice offering me the opportunity to press 1, 2, 3, or 4? *Not.* Those systems may be convenient and save time for your established clients to get answers, but they can be roadblocks to new clients trying to do business with you.

Compare the value of the clients you keep (and keep happy) against what you invest in a very polite person to answer your phones and provide immediate verbal assistance.

LOYALTY-BUILDING CAMPAIGNS

If you're looking for loyalty-building ideas, it's wise to learn from other companies who are doing it successfully. Start with companies you find yourself loyal to. What do they do for you above and beyond providing the products or services you purchase? How often do they get their information in front of you? In what manner?

Some companies with strong reputations for client retention (loyalty) include: L.L.Bean, Omaha Steaks, Harry & David, Sears, and insurance providers such as State Farm, Nationwide, and Aflac. Please note that I don't mean to say that any company not listed here is doing a poor job of retention. These are just a few with good reputations that came to mind.

There are also product *brands* that we find ourselves loyal to. Do you buy a certain brand of peanut butter? Is it because you like it, because it's economical, or because

Mom always bought it? Do you drive a particular make of vehicle because Dad always drove that kind and it's familiar to you? Where does your loyalty come from? Gaining insight into your own loyalties should help you with ideas for building it with your clients.

If you're still not certain what would work to build loyalty among your clients, consider involving them in the process. Many companies conduct surveys of their existing clients to find out what motivates those clients to continue doing business with them. Surveys are great tools. You can simply ask questions like, "How are we doing?" Or ask questions about specific offers or product add-ons you may be considering in the future. It's a great way to test the waters for something new.

One of the benefits of surveys, in particular if you use an online tool, is that you can generate an overall report showing pie charts and other forms of analysis of the answers. It's best to keep your surveys short—six to ten questions. During challenging times people won't want to and shouldn't be asked to invest much of their time doing something for you.

Note: If you're going to use a survey, you'll get more responses if you offer a gift or reward to those who reply. It can be something you offer online, or a physical item that is shipped after the survey results are in. Just make certain it's something of real value to your clients.

Properly worded questions can generate answers that tell you what's going on in their business; the impact the current challenges may have on them during the next eighteen to twenty-four months; their plans to weather the storm or to stay on top; and whether or not they anticipate downsizing, placing smaller orders, or keeping the status quo.

You need to be careful what you ask in an online survey, because they can be somewhat impersonal. If you're a small business with few clients, you'd be better off conducting the survey yourself. You won't have the same reporting features as the software provides, but you may get better answers. If you're doing a survey by phone, I suggest you narrow your questions down to two or three and tell your clients that you *"have three quick questions to ask."* Always demonstrate that you value their time.

If appropriate for your industry and product, you might want to invite a small group of clients in noncompeting fields together for a luncheon and hold a round-table discussion about the changes in the economy or how your products might better serve their needs. Many of my students have found this a tremendous resource, and their clients formed networking relationships as a side benefit of the gathering. And who was the hero for setting that up? The salesperson. It was a win-win-*win* situation.

It's a privilege to serve the needs of others. Take it seriously. Always remember that other vendors are trying to capture your clients from you just as you're going after theirs. Appreciate your clients and treat them right, and they'll remain loyal to you and your company.

Start by Keeping the Business You Have

SUMMARY

- You understand that loyalty is built over time and by giving consistent attention to your clients.
- You end every client meeting with these words: *"Is there anything else I can do for you?"*
- You have multiple ideas for building client loyalty through phone calls, e-mail, and postal mail.
- You know how to approach a neglected client to regain their trust and keep their business.
- You will begin a study of other companies that have loyal clients and incorporate some of their strategies into your business.

6. Success Is in Who You Already Know

In the business world, unwise men take more than they give. They do not realize that they are breaking the Universal Law which will eventually break them to an equal extent. It may not be balanced in the form of dollars and cents but in the loss of good-will upon which their future business depends.

—Walter Russell

When faced with challenging times, you need to look with fresh eyes at those things that have been around you all along. What does that mean? Knowing that you need to keep as many clients as you possibly can, you want to give each one special attention. Review your history with each of them and their current account statuses. Look for changes in their ordering patterns to gain ideas of how you can better serve them. Mentally put yourself in their shoes in order to see things from their perspective.

If you offer a product that's used by a whole company—such as software, or printers and copiers—you may want to get permission to spend a day in their offices. Shadowing some of their heavy users of your product could help you see other ways to assist them. While your key contact may be Sally in accounting, Carol in HR uses the same software program and could benefit from a little added training with it. You won't find that out, though, unless you get an opportunity to see how Carol uses it. And Carol may know HR directors at other companies to whom she could refer you—especially when she gains new insight into the other advantages of using your product.

Consider the products and services each client company has acquired from you in the past. Are there alternatives available that might be more economical so they can still order the quantities they've ordered before but save money? Or, if they're ordering smaller quantities, might this be a time for them to test a higher-quality product—keeping the dollar amount of their orders the same? You don't know unless you ask, do you?

It could be that your clients haven't taken a good look at their ordering patterns in a while and your analysis could trigger some changes. Of course there's always a risk that the changes will be that they'll order less, but you, the sales pro, will not just give them the analysis and let them draw their own conclusions. Your analysis will include suggestions for testing higher-quality products (with bigger profit margins) or even adding some new ones to their current orders.

Expand your thinking to include how you can serve their needs beyond your product offering. What's happening in your industry or your other clients' industries that might be helpful for all your clients to know? Of course, you wouldn't share any competitive secrets or information. However, if John's Auto Sales is finding success in the current market with postcard mailings, it would be okay to tell Sally's Quilt Shoppe about it.

Hopefully, reviewing your notes will stimulate a recollection of your conversations with the people at each client company. Was something said about a competing company or one of this company's clients while you waited in the lobby for your meeting? How about as you worked on developing rapport with the purchasing agent? Does anything that was said then make you now wonder who else this client knows?

Even if Bill and Sue Consumer gave you several referrals when you made the initial sale to them, if they're like most clients they're meeting new people all the time. Have you stayed in touch with them and provided good service? Do you talk with them about what's happening in their lives, or do you stick strictly to business topics? Who knows, they may have joined a new health club or social group and met a bunch of new people you could network with through them. Have you continued to ask for quality introductions to potential new clients?

The phrase *quality introductions* is something I've taught for a number of years. In essence, it's earning the right to ask for referrals to the friends, relatives, and business associates of existing clients. But instead of just asking for the names and contact information of those people, you set the stage differently by asking for introductions. The mental picture you create is different, and in selling, this kind of different is good.

As an example, picture yourself at a party. You're talking with your acquaintance Kathy about how your business is doing. She nods toward another woman across the room and says, *"Marsha has an interest in that. In fact, she works with X-Co. They use those types of products."* You've just been given a referral opportunity. You could walk right up to Marsha, introduce yourself and say, *"Hi, my name is Kevin. I was just talking to Kathy and she told me . . . ,"* and try to start a conversation.

How much better would it be if you ask Kathy to walk over to Marsha with you and make the introduction? She already knows Marsha, and Marsha will lower her guard more than she would with you, a perfect stranger approaching her and using Kathy's name. Kathy is now in essence approaching, with her existing good relationship with Marsha in tow . . . and you . . . almost as if your introduction to her is a gift. *"Hi, Marsha. It's good to see you. I was just talking with Kevin here and he mentioned that his company does X. I know you are familiar with that, so I thought I'd introduce you. Marsha, this is Kevin Perkins. Kevin, Marsha Taylor."* And you take it from there.

The same thing can be done over the telephone. When an appropriate subject comes up about business, and Mike tells you he recently met Carl, who uses your type of service, you get as many details as you can about Carl. Then, ask Mike if he'd be willing to introduce you to Carl. If he's a satisfied client, he'll be happy to. All he needs to do is make a quick call to let Carl know he asked you to contact him. Nothing more needs to be said.

Mike doesn't need to try to sell Carl your product. In

fact, you want to discourage Mike from telling too much about the product or service . . . just have him tell Carl what a great guy (or gal) you are. Mike will never do the product justice. All you should expect him to say is that it's wonderful and how much it's saved his company, increased his business, or whatever it does. It's your job to sell the product. His part, if he's willing to help you, is to open the door for you with the quality introduction.

Isn't a quality introduction so much better than trying to make the connection on your own? You may be surprised to learn how many Kathys and Mikes there are in the world who don't even realize how many people they know unless and until you start asking. And they're more than happy to introduce you around. It makes them feel good to do it. When Kathy introduces two people to each other and it works out for the best, her reputation grows and more people want to know her. It's an outward spiral of opportunity.

When a purchasing agent, Robert, moves up in the company, it's likely he'll get to know people in other departments or branches that you might serve. Remember to stay in touch with him, but probably less often than his successor, who is now handling the purchasing from you. You don't want the new purchasing agent to think you're going over his or her head by talking with Robert after he moves to his new position. But, don't let the past goodwill with Robert die on the vine, either.

Does it now make sense to you that if John and Mary belong to Group X, they are meeting other people like themselves who need your product? If you've been serving John and Mary's needs quite well since gaining their business, it's likely they'll be willing to make an introduction for you. You just need to ask.

Remember our lesson from a previous chapter and be certain to *give something* before you *ask*. *Give* excellent service. *Give* a creative idea they may benefit from. *Give* valuable information. *Give* quality introductions.

Always keep in mind quality introductions you can make for your clients. Be a "Kathy," as in our previous example. If you can create concentric circles of influence around yourself, where you are constantly meeting new people and helping them by introducing them to others, you'll find the positive backlash from that *service* bringing you almost more business than you can handle—in any economic condition.

Compare this to getting on the A list of Hollywood parties. You travel in the highest orbit. You meet the right people, and it all works for the good of everyone involved. People in your circle know, like, and trust you. So when you make quality introductions they're taken seriously, and the new acquaintances treat each other with a certain level of respect that makes for faster and often better new relationships for everyone involved. It's a win-win-win, and you created it!

WHEN YOUR COMPANY GOES OUT OF BUSINESS OR DOWNSIZES

When faced with challenges in an industry or the overall economy, things have to change. People and businesses must adapt. Too many people fear change because they see only the negative side of it. Hopefully, that's not the case with you. It may sound trite, but we all need to embrace change. Change is the only way we get better. To borrow a quote from the late, great motivational speaker, Earl Nightingale, "*If you're not moving forward in business, you're developing the first signs of death. The same law applies to you, personally.*"

"Moving forward" involves change. Okay, so maybe having it forced upon us or being blindsided by it isn't fun, but when you're a true professional in your industry, this should only happen to you on a rare occasion. If you've taken the information you've read up to this point in the book to heart, you'll be one of those on the front of the wave of change. You'll see it coming as it hits the horizon and put yourself in a position to ride that wave safely to shore.

In Earl Nightingale's incredible audio recording *Lead the Field*, he suggests that we are all ultimately the presidents of our own personal corporations. He goes on to say that our primary job is to increase the value of our company stock each and every year. To do so requires that we constantly change and grow.

I strongly encourage you to not only read and apply the information in this book, but to continue to read, listen to audio programs (like *Lead the Field*), attend seminars or webinars, or take classes—especially those covering communication skills—to improve your effectiveness in business on a regular basis. If you get just one great idea from a lecture or book that helps you build better relationships with your clients, it's well worth the investment of time and money.

Unfortunately, there are always a few businesses that

don't make the cut for whatever reason. They may have large overheads, or they've lost a large client whose orders made up most of their sales. Their industry may have taken a hit and they were unprepared to adapt.

Today's swift pace of product development makes existing products obsolete so fast at times it can make your head spin. Unprepared salespeople think it'll never happen to them. They are taken by surprise by the competition and forced to start over elsewhere. If you market something that's considered a trendy product, you'll likely see change coming swiftly and surely. In fields where demand is more solidly based and growth has been steady, a slower course of change is more likely.

No matter how it happens, it does. Hopefully, your business isn't one of those that closes its doors. If it is, you need to evaluate your position and your reputation in your field or community. If you've always been one of the good guys with healthy sales records, your services will likely be in demand by a surviving company. Smart survivors will let a lesser achiever go to take on a proven entity. That's why they're survivors.

When seeking new employment, don't operate from the standpoint of where you'll be getting your next paycheck. You need to consider where you will find yourself most valued because of your experience and your client relationships. You want to work for a company that appreciates its salespeople; a company that is planning for the future and has new products coming online.

Many businesses will ask their salespeople not to work for competing businesses should they leave. Some even have the proper legal wording in their hiring agreements. However, those clauses might become null and void if the business goes under. You need to be 100 percent certain of where you stand should this happen. If you enjoy your industry and want to work for a surviving competitor, you must be standing on solid ground legally. Otherwise you'll do both yourself and your industry harm in the long run.

If your company closes its doors and you are able to work for a competitor, don't just jump on board the first ship that passes by. Consider your clients: (1) What company will best serve their needs if they follow you? (2) *Will* they follow you?

Hopefully, you know in advance of any major changes in your company—like its going out of business, discontinuing a product line, or closing a local office. If it's appropriate and legal to do so, you will want to forewarn your clients only of changes that affect them. In the case of the company closing, assure them that you intend to land on your feet and continue to work in the industry with a quality company. If you've provided them with good service, they may tell you to let them know where you go so they can follow. It would save them a lot of time and hassle in finding a new supplier of their own and training a new sales rep to handle their particular needs.

If you can't talk with them in advance of the change, be prepared to contact them as soon as it is possible to do so. Undoubtedly, word will be out among your competitors that your company won't be around long, and they'll be chomping at the bit to try to pick up your orphaned clients—with or without you.

If you've told your clients that you work only with the best company, that's great. However, if you've been less than professional and knocked the competition, then have to find a job among those formerly competing companies, how would that look? In a situation like that, your clients will likely start looking on their own for a better company to work with—and a more professional representative.

If you seek new employment with the company that's most likely to survive the current tough times, be certain that they also provide a decent product. Your clients will still have needs for that type of product if your current company goes under. If you do your due diligence and determine that it's a good choice, your clients will probably make the switch with you. You'll have the benefit of starting at a new company with an existing client base. Even if the fee structure is different from that of your old company, your income shouldn't take too hard a hit because of your smart transition.

When making a change because your old company closed, think about what you bring to a new company—your experience, your product and industry knowledge, and your clients. During your due-diligence phase, it's wise to let your potential new employer know your past track record, of course. However, you also want to give them a rough idea of what percentage of your past clients may make the move with you. You can use that somewhat as a bargaining chip in getting the best product for those old clients and possibly a signing bonus for yourself. Only do this if you truly believe the new company has an excellent replacement product to offer. As with any negotiations in a sales career, ethics always come first!

WHEN THE COMPETITION GOES DOWN

Where do all those clients of the competition go when a company closes? Unless their salespeople are as good as you in helping them make the transition to a new supplier, those clients may flounder for a bit. They'll have to invest time and effort in researching new sources. If you work with a company that's going to survive, you want to do everything in your power to pick up those clients. Hopefully, your company will be hiring some of the closing competitor's top sales guns, who might bring them along. If your company is not in a position to take on new overhead but wants the client business, it may be up to you to start networking with those salespeople to get a foot in the door (or at least a few names of good clients). You may already know who some of those clients are because you were unable to win their business in the past.

Perhaps your company could come up with some creative way to compensate those former competitor's salespeople with referral fees if they swing that business your way. Again, ethics come into play here, and everyone needs to play fair to avoid any legal or other ramifications.

How do you approach those clients? Carefully. Hopefully, they'll see you as the answer to their prayers or as arriving on a white steed and ready to get down to business. They'll appreciate your reaching out to them, knowing they were either in a bind or left in the lurch by the competition.

Some may be a bit leery of doing business with you, depending on what caused the competitor to go out of business and how much they may have suffered because of it. They aren't going to want to start up with your company and face the same issue six months from now. They'll need to know you plan to be in business long enough to truly help them. They won't be willing to put their loyalty on the line anytime soon. With those folks you'll have to work harder to gain their trust, and you may have to start with small orders to prove how well you will serve their needs.

One idea for approaching them is a modification of the objection-handling strategy called, "Put the shoe on their foot." With this approach you ask them how they would handle this situation if they were in your shoes or in your company's position: *"Mr. Parker, I'd like to tell you that I understand your situation completely—your fear of making a commitment to my company, especially since you just went through a challenge with my predecessor. But, I have never been exactly in your shoes. Knowing what you know today, if you were the owner of my company, facing a potential client who had a bad past experience, how would you suggest the situation be handled?"* Then, listen for the answer. Mr. Parker will tell you exactly how he wants to be treated. Then, when you treat him that way, you've earned his business.

GETTING INTRODUCTIONS FROM NONCLIENTS

To this point in the book, you've learned many ways to approach existing clients to generate leads for new business. Now, let's cover some ideas for getting introductions from people who are not your clients.

Unless you're in the funeral business, there's bound to be a large group of people you know who would not be likely to benefit from your product or use your service. Do yourself a favor and do not count them out. It's a small world. If you haven't experienced this yet, I hope you do soon. Everyone you know has other friends and acquaintances besides you. So, even if they're not a candidate for your product, they may very well know someone who is.

Even if you sell private jets and your potential client list is relatively small, someone you know probably knows someone who can get you a lead or an introduction. At the time I'm writing this book, a little over ten thousand private jets fly across the United States on a regular basis. Needless to say, the potential client list for small jet aircraft is somewhat exclusive. However, if you can tap into the exclusive level by way of a potential client's child's soccer coach, massage therapist, or grandma, you want to do it.

Even if your immediate family members and friends don't directly know people who may be interested in your product or service, they know people who know people. It's your job to stay tuned into what's going on in their lives and the circles in which they operate. You need to plant seeds with others constantly for word of a connection to someone who would be a good match to your product or service.

When you're speaking with anyone in your circle of acquaintances, simply ask, *"Who do you know that enjoys the RV lifestyle?"* Don't ask "Do you know anyone?" That type of question more often than not leads to the same answer, "No, I don't." When you ask "Who do you know?" the other person's mind does a different type of search in their brain. The answers to *who* questions require thought. So do the answers to *what, when, where,* and *why* questions. Questions with easy answers like yes and no will give you only those answers, so avoid them when trying to get someone to picture the face of a potential referral or to pull a name from their memory banks.

Ask the same questions of the proprietors and staff at the businesses you frequent. Everyone in the world is approachable. Your job is to make the right approach.

My mentor, J. Douglas Edwards, used to tell a story about a professional baseball player who was traded to a different team. The details of the trade were all over the local news of the city where he was to move. It was a big topic of conversation. Few people in the area didn't know about him having a young family and a very high salary. This included the local salespeople. Yet few even gave a second thought to trying to get his business.

A local real estate salesperson sent the player a note of congratulations on the trade and welcomed him to the new community. He included his business card and offered to answer any questions the player might have about the area.

Guess what? He was the only real estate agent to contact that young player. They called, and he helped that family find a suitable property. As most real estate agents will do, he also prepared a list of local insurance vendors, information on schools, shopping, churches, and so forth. He became a key contact for that player. He earned a good fee for service on the real estate sale and generated quite a bit of referral business for those on his list.

WHOSE LIST ARE YOU ON?

If you don't already have a referral list of your own to offer your clients the services of other quality professionals in appropriate noncompeting industries, create one. And get everyone you put on that list to create one and include you on it. You never know where that list may end up . . . hopefully, in the hands of qualified clients that you didn't have to seek out yourself. Isn't that your favorite kind of call? *"Hello, my name is Angie Smith. I got your name from my real estate agent/pest control company/ dry cleaner/boss. I need . . ."*

It's likely that Angie is prequalified and will have a lowered wall of sales resistance. She has your name from someone she trusts, even if you've never served that person's needs. Take care of Angie. Then call the person who gave her your name and let them know what happened. Thank them for the referral. If they're not already a client, go for a counterreferral and use Angie's satisfaction with your service to open the door with this person.

THE POWER OF POSITIVE PRESS

In 2008 basketball great Shaquille O'Neal started playing for my home NBA team, the Phoenix Suns. He drove a very large truck, suitable for the big man that he is. Unfortunately, there were not many large parking spaces in the dense retail areas around many of the local restaurants. Shaq was meeting someone for lunch one hot summer day (over 100 degrees) and found that he had to park several blocks from the restaurant. A fan had recognized him and said hello. He asked the fan for a lift over to the restaurant. The fan was amazed at the request and gladly agreed. The newsworthy part was that the fan was driving a compact vehicle that Shaq had a hard time fitting into. The fan took a photo of Shaq in his tiny car and Shaq picked the fan up for another photo. The photos and story made the local interest section of the newspaper.

While many readers of that article were commenting on how fun it must have been to meet Shaq and do him a favor, my thoughts ran to opportunity. If I were a restaurant owner in that area reading the article, I would have sent a message to Shaq that if he would like to dine in my restaurant, I'd reserve an appropriate-sized parking spot close by for him to park his oversized vehicle. Or, if that wasn't doable, I'd offer to send a car for him. I'd even offer as secluded a table as I could provide and a private entrance or exit if he so desired. The notoriety of having Shaq as a patron would undoubtedly boost my business. My good deed would reap many rewards and might even make the news as well.

I try to steer my students away from reading the gloom-and-doom news on a regular basis. However, if you do make reading the newspaper a habit, read every newsworthy item with an eye to opportunity. It's there, but only you will recognize what will work for you, your product, and your industry.

EXPAND YOUR CIRCLE

What groups or organizations do you currently belong to? Membership and participation in civic or industry groups can get you some great exposure. You will be recognized as a viable supporter of the group. People will feel more confident about talking with you than if you were a complete stranger. If you're very active in an industry group, that helps build your credibility as an expert. People you may not now know will be drawn to you when they have questions about your area of expertise.

Are you involved with the local chamber of commerce? How about Toastmasters? Those are two of the best organizations I know of for networking opportunities. Networking, done right, will provide you with some wonderful business leads from new sources.

How do you "do networking" right? First of all, you prepare. When you meet someone new, it's standard procedure to ask for a name and find out what type of business they're in.

I find it interesting that most of us define ourselves by what we do, not necessarily by who we are. As an example, consider a small group where people have come together for a specific purpose. The leader of the group will most likely have each person introduce themselves and tell a little about their backgrounds or why they are there. You hear things like this: *"My name is Joseph Callaghan. I am an attorney, and I'm here today because . . ." "I'm Martha Patterson. My kids attend this, so I'm here to help."* We tend to identify ourselves by what we do or who we're related to.

In sales, you want to master the strategy of identifying yourself by the service you provide. Never again tell someone you have just met that you're a salesperson for ABC Company. Tell them the benefits you provide. *"I'm Tom Hopkins. I help businesses increase sales, thus their bottom lines, by enhancing the experience clients have with their firms."* If I had said, "I'm a sales trainer," people would have preconceived notions about my profession. By describing the service I provide, I create curiosity to know more, which leads to new people wanting to make my acquaintance.

Here are some other examples of benefit descriptions to help you get a better idea. After you read through them, write your own. Memorize it. And, start using it.

Financial Services: *"I show people ways to make and save money. We have a wonderful way of analyzing where people are today, where they were in the past, and how to get where they want to be in the future, based on their financial dreams and goals. It's an exciting program."*

Home Improvements: *"I help people maintain and improve the value of what is very likely their single largest investment. As an example, if I could send you home with a magic wand and you could stand out in front of your home and wave it to change any one thing about your home, other than the mortgage, what would it be?"*

Real Estate: *"I show people how to take their dreams of living in their own home, creating memories with their loved ones, and turn them into reality."*

Backyard Environments: *"I'm a fun expert. I help families have more fun time together in their own backyards."*

The descriptions are not about the products. They're about the benefits.

When selecting groups to be involved with, consider both your skills in business and your talents with nonbusiness interests or hobbies. You don't necessarily have to join ten different groups and attend endless meetings to participate. Many organizations have volunteer opportunities for non-members. Do what you can. Do a good deed and meet new people along the way. Where do you find these opportunities? Typically, they're printed in the newspaper and posted on group Web sites. If you aren't sure where to start, ask around in your existing circle of friends and acquaintances. If you put the word out that you're seeking volunteer opportunities, people will be glad to help you get involved.

Be certain to achieve the goal of the group before attempting to talk with other members with regard to your product or service. Also, be appreciative of everyone in your developing network. If you are cautious about not taking advantage of them, they'll be all the more open to helping you. Going back to an earlier point, end every conversation with them by asking what you can do for them.

SUMMARY

- You will review your current client files and order history, seeking new ideas to keep or expand their business.
- You understand the power of asking for quality introductions rather than leads.
- You never make a call or contact to *ask* for something unless you have something to *give*.
- If your company goes under, you won't panic. You know how to move on from a position of strength.
- You have a unique approach to potential new clients who have been orphaned by another company's closing.
- You will research local groups you could participate in or volunteer opportunities where you'll help others, get some exposure, and meet new people.
- You have written a description of the benefits you offer people/companies to use when meeting new people.

7. How to Quickly Determine If Someone Is an Ideal New Client for You

A professional knows when his or her most effective presentation is not to give one. They learn this in qualifying.

—Tom Hopkins

This could very well be the most important chapter in the entire book as far as skill building. Proper qualifying of potential clients is where average salespeople cut corners and the pros never do.

What is the qualifying step of the selling process? If you're a pro, it's the step after making your initial contact and before presenting any of your products as solutions. If you attempt to qualify before establishing rapport, you'll come across as too abrupt and possibly even greedy. If you do it too late in the presentation, you may find that you've done a lot of work for nothing.

Qualification needs to happen early in the selling cycle so you don't find yourself spinning your wheels with someone who cannot make a purchase. It's where you ask questions to determine the needs of your potential clients. You then mentally match their needs to your products and services. If you come up with a solid match, you then secondarily qualify them as to how soon they would want to apply a solution to their needs and what they can afford.

Qualifying is the turning point in your selling cycle. One of two things happens: (1) you determine this new contact is qualified and move smoothly into the next step of presentation; or (2) you determine they're not qualified and you gracefully move on to another potential client.

The more qualified the potential client is, the more likely it is that you'll close the sale. A qualified client does not, however, *guarantee* a closed sale. Getting the final decision is totally up to you and your skills at presenting, addressing concerns, and closing—all of which happen after qualification.

Referred leads are usually the most qualified. It will, hopefully, be a rare case where someone gives you a referral to a client who is totally unqualified for your product or service. Of course they may not know how the person they're referring would answer your qualifying questions, but in most cases they're giving you the contact information for someone who is a lot like them. Since they had a need for your offering, it's likely the other folks will have one too.

People who are referred to you hear of you from someone else who is already happy with your product or service. It's likely that they trust that satisfied client and there's a certain level of trust that transfers from that relationship to you. Referrals typically think they'd enjoy the same benefits as the referrer and so are quite open to talking with you.

Be careful not to assume you can take shortcuts with qualifying these folks, though. Just because they think they're like one of your existing clients doesn't mean they are. The Maxwells and the Parkers might live on the same street in the same type of home and have similar work histories. But the Maxwells might be better at managing their spending and be able to afford your offering. The Parkers may be in over their heads with debt and not be financially qualified, even though your product meets a perceived need.

This is the only time in the entire selling cycle that you need your clients to do most of the talking. The more they talk, the more you learn about whether or not you can help them. This is not to say that you switch to lecture mode after qualifying them, but that your job in this step of the selling cycle is to lead them with questions. Get them to open up about their needs, wants, hopes, dreams, and financial situations.

It's important to realize that few people or companies make drastic changes in their buying habits. They tend to buy the same brands, similar products—maybe with some upgrades or stylish new colors. So it's important to ask questions about their past purchases of products like yours. Get them talking about their buying experiences (good or bad), details about the products they have owned, and what they liked about those products.

Then ask questions about why they're now considering

change. Ask what more or what different things they expect in a new product. Their answers will tell you what their expectations are. If you do a good job here, they'll pretty much tell you exactly what they want to own and the price range they would be comfortable with. That's why it's so critical to the success of your overall career to be good at this step.

Be careful in listening for what we call their hot buttons. These are features they would not want to do without. Too many average salespeople get caught up in selling what they like to sell rather than what the clients want to own. These hot buttons fly right by them, and they fail to use them wisely in their presentations.

If there's a feature or an option that your client absolutely must have and you don't offer it, you must proceed carefully. You may have to help them weigh the value of that feature against all the others that you can provide. If the benefits of all the other features are great enough, they may consider moving forward without that one hot button. In fact, they may realize it isn't that important, after all. Perhaps it was a feature on all past models of the product, so they were used to having it but never gave its value a second thought. In some cases, you'll be able to win them over. In many, you won't.

I had a buyer once who insisted he wanted a home with hardwood floors. In my area there weren't any newer homes with hardwood floors, and some of the older homes with wood floors had other flaws or were poorly designed. I did some research on what it would cost to replace the floors in a newer home with hardwood if I was able to find a floor plan he might like. I also looked into those older homes. I was prepared to work with him either way, but we started by viewing the older homes with his "hot button" hardwood floors. In the end, the client did purchase one of the older homes, sticking to his original plan, but did some major renovation to the home's structure over the next few years. If I had tried to push him into one of the newer homes, suggesting he redo the floors, I may have lost the sale, any referral business, and his future business.

WHERE TO FIND QUALIFIED CLIENTS

Prequalified leads are the best. They may have been referred to you by an existing client, or you may find them as part of a group or demographic that you already serve. Hopefully, you keep track of how you first come in contact with each client. That way, when things are slow, you can go back to that same source for more potential clients. It's likely that if one good, qualified client was found in a certain way or place, more of the same will come from that source.

As human beings we tend to hang around with people who are very much like us. It's where we're comfortable. Think about it. Don't you hang out with friends and neighbors, parents of your kids' friends, and so on? You belong to groups or associations where you'll find other businesspeople like yourself. You may be at similar stages of your lives or careers, have similar interests and goals.

Doesn't it seem probable, then, that the source of your most qualified clients probably has more of the same awaiting your attention? Where was it that you first met Mr. Orders-a-lot or Ms. Frequent Purchaser? Was it a chance meeting at a party? Whose party was it? Were they referred by someone else? Did you get their name from a list? Did they call your company? Was it from an ad or were they just shopping and found you?

By knowing where your existing clients came from, you can create a list of likely places to gain potential new leads for more business. When times are tough, it's in your best interest to serve more clients. Of course you need to keep your current clients happy, but if they're placing smaller orders, you'll need a larger client base to keep your income where you want it to be.

It's also important to have a clear demographic description of your ideal clients. Start by writing out a list of criteria of who makes a good client for you.

If you sell to consumers, are they of a certain age range? Married? Single? With or without children? Do they travel abroad? Live in a certain community? Drive trucks or sports cars? Are they alumni from a Big Ten university? Do they work in any specific field (such as doctors, lawyers, dentists, architects, blue-collar, etc.)? Are they outdoor enthusiasts? Do they camp, hunt, or fish?

If your products are used by businesses, are they in 12,000+-square-foot buildings? Are they manufacturing plants, retail locations, or offices? What are their typical usage requirements?

You get the idea. You can either generate your list based on your many qualified and satisfied clients or, if you're rather new to selling, start with the benefits of your

products. Think *"My clients are people who need
_____."* Create your list of the five or six top criteria you find most of your clients have.

1. _____

2. _____

3. _____

4. _____

5. _____

6. _____

Watch for patterns that emerge when compiling this list. You may find that you've walked by hundreds if not thousands of dollars of potential business and not realized they were probably qualified to own what you offer.

Let's compare this to shopping for a new vehicle. Once you decide you want a red truck, you seem to see red trucks everywhere, don't you? In reality, they were there all along. You just didn't have "red truck" as a criterion when watching the world go by.

Once your list is compiled, memorize it! Then, when someone mentions any of these criteria, your mind should register, *Hey, that person (or company) might be qualified to own my product. I'm going to stop what I'm doing and learn more about them.* You'll soon find yourself walking toward more opportunities rather than passing them by.

Using these criteria as a measure will also help you spot people who may not be qualified to own your product or service. You know what I mean. You start a conversation with someone and they mention several things . . . maybe those on your list . . . that would make them qualified to get involved with your service. But then, one or two other points that come up show that they aren't truly good candidates now. (Like the fact that they're experiencing their worst quarter of their fiscal year.) However, they may be qualified in six months or even two years. So, you don't go into your full-blown presentation, but you do keep the door open to future business with them. Keeping this list fresh in your mind helps you to become more effective at maximizing your selling time and capturing information on potential future clients, as well.

GETTING POTENTIAL CLIENTS TO TALK

To learn more about whether or not they're qualified to own your product or enjoy the benefits of your service, you need to get the people you come in contact with to talk. As we mentioned before, you do that by asking questions. But what are the best questions to ask to get the information you need? Simply put: the ones that give you the information you need.

I teach a reverse qualification method that we'll use here. Rather than looking at the selling step of qualification from the *before* scenario, let's look at it from *after*.

What do you know about someone who is an extremely well-qualified client for your product or service? Think of some of your most satisfied clients. What key points helped them and you realize working together was a win-win situation?

This goes beyond the criteria listed above. Think of some past situations where you were filling out your paperwork or entering order information on your computer. You were feeling pretty happy to be serving their needs. They were happy to have made the decision. What questions helped steer you toward offering a particular product? What about that product was ideal for serving that client's needs?

Take a moment and list the ideal information you would know about someone before guiding them to own just one of your most popular products. Do it right here in the book so you have your notes as we proceed.

_____

_____

_____

_____

_____

Now, let's work backward. What questions would you ask to get that information? What order makes the most sense? To know whether or not you're on the right track, ask yourself this about each question: *"Will the answer to this question tell me if this prospective client actually has the need, desire, and financial wherewithal to make a decision today if my product is the best one for their needs?"* If your questions do not lead you to answer yes, you're not qualifying to the best of your ability.

———————————————————————————

———————————————————————————

———————————————————————————

———————————————————————————

———————————————————————————

———————————————————————————

Give yourself some time to work on this. Fine-tune the questions until they feel comfortable. Once you get it right, your sales process will go so much more smoothly. The questions need to be conversational yet pointed . . . in the direction of getting the sale.

One note of caution: It's important not to come across as someone running through a checklist of questions during your sales calls, like it's a drill of some sort, or a game of Twenty Questions. Your tone must be professional, conversational.

You need to gain a clear understanding of where each client is coming from and what they want to move toward. In sales it's just as important that you address features a client wouldn't use or need as it is to address those your clients will enjoy. The desire for change can be to move away from something that's not working just as it can be to move toward something new that fulfills a need. Both aspects help to point you toward what they are interested in owning.

Once you understand and use this strategy for a single product, invest some nonselling time in doing it for other products you offer. The better prepared you are, the easier you'll find the qualification process. And the faster you'll find yourself moving into powerful presentations. The better (and more pointed) your presentation, the stronger your closing ratio will be.

THE POWER OF EFFECTIVE QUALIFYING

Knowing how to properly, effectively, and quickly qualify potential clients is the step in the selling cycle that makes the difference between having an average income and achieving Champion status in your company, your area, or your industry. Years ago, we worked with an industrial psychologist who was developing an evaluation tool to test the selling skills of applicants. After testing his system on over 250,000 sales professionals, he proved this point— knowing how to qualify makes a bigger difference in your bottom line than does knowing how to close. Those with strong qualifying skills were more likely than not to have earned six-figure incomes.

Of course, if you have a highly qualified client and you never ask for the order, you won't close, but too many sales-people waste selling time spinning their wheels with nonqualified clients. For that reason they don't earn the higher incomes that the Champion qualifiers do.

The purpose of a sound qualifying strategy is to economize on time—yours *and* theirs. You don't want to invest your valuable selling time with people who aren't qualified to own your product. They don't want to invest time talking with you if there's nothing in it for them.

You will occasionally run into folks with nothing better to do and an interest in your product line even if they're not qualified to own it. Your strategy for these folks is to be pleasant and kind. Gently offer to send them some information, rather than investing face time or phone time with them. As mentioned before, even though they may not be qualified to own your product, they may know others who are.

I don't mean to sound callous here, but selling is truly a matter of numbers. You need to master the step of qualification and quickly (though not in a brusque manner) determine if each lead you have acquired is truly a good potential candidate.

If they are not qualified, you want to be pleasant and leave the door open to future business in case things change for them, but move along. Before you leave any unqualified client, though, determine if they know anyone else who might be a candidate for your product and go for that referral. Situations can change rapidly. Sara may not be qualified today to hire your catering service, but she may receive a bonus next month or an inheritance and want to celebrate with a special gathering. You always want to leave a positive impression with nonclients so they will think of you when the time is right for them.

If this company or these people are good candidates for your product, you then go deeper into qualifying their needs to determine the best solution to present to them. We talked about this in chapter 4. You gather as much information as possible about their needs, then summarize before presenting your solution.

In some instances, you may meet a qualified client in a nonbusiness situation. It's not likely that the timing will be conducive to going further with them at that time. Your sales goal for those situations is not to go deeper into qualifying and preparing to present. Rather, it's to close for a time to discuss how the benefits of your product will serve their needs. The challenge here is to meet with them while their interest is high and before anything changes that might make them less qualified—like the competition getting to them first.

When I was in real estate, I used to hold open houses on properties. It never failed that a good, qualified client would come through the door. The home where the open house was would not have been right for them, but I couldn't leave it to show them other, more suitable properties. They were ready to own. I couldn't run off to serve their needs without leaving my open-house client in the lurch.

Eventually, I came up with a solution for this situation. I started bringing half-gallon containers of ice cream to my open houses. If I determined someone was going to be a good client for me but not for that property, I would get their contact information, offer to show them properties as soon as possible, and give them a half-gallon of ice cream as a gift. Where were they going on a warm summer day with a half-gallon of ice cream? In most cases, they were going home to either eat it or put it in their freezer. It was my way of keeping them from viewing additional properties without me.

THE PRODUCT WILL SERVE THEIR NEEDS, BUT ARE THEY READY TO OWN?

Actually, there's one more step in the qualification strategy that can make all the difference. Once you have the information on their needs, ask if they're ready to own. Be careful here. This is much different from asking a closing question—asking for the order. At this stage of the presentation, you are qualifying them as to their ability and desire to make a buying decision *now* as opposed to six months from now. Yet you're not asking them for that actual decision. You can't. You haven't presented a solution yet!

Here are some suggestions as to how you might handle this situation:

"Mr. Jackson, if we are fortunate to find the right solution for you today, how soon would you want to begin using the forklift?" Some clients may love what you have to offer and be qualified but just not ready now. They may have a date six months in the future when they would start using your product. They may have to get it included in the budget for the next fiscal year. By then, you may have a different pricing structure or even a new product line, depending on what business you're in. You need to know what their time frame is before investing a lot of time in presenting today's solution.

"Barb, what is the procedure for making a final decision for starting a new service such as ours?" Barb may be the point person for a committee. The committee may meet only once a month. You want to know this before giving your finest presentation. Rather than giving it all to Barb, you would need to present to the entire group. All you're going to try to sell Barb on today is getting in front of the group at the next meeting.

When it comes to committees, you want to learn who is on the committee and each of their positions. The opinions of some may weigh more heavily than others. You want to know this as you prepare your presentation. For example, if you learn that Scott Baker in the finance department has the final say after the committee has made their choice, you'd better prepare the financial aspect of your presentation extremely well. If Madeline Paxton in the creative department has the final say, you will want your presentation to be graphically appealing.

When you reach the presentation stage and have more than one person operating in the decision-maker capacity, it's very important to make good eye contact with everyone in the room. If you're selling to consumers in their homes and little Johnny is sitting on Mom's lap, you want to include him as well. Otherwise, he may decide he needs to be the center of Mom's attention, and you've lost control.

Here's another example of how to ask if they're ready to make a decision: *"Mike, if everything we're covering here makes sense are you in a position to proceed?"* If your products require financing of any type, Mike may need to qualify for a loan before being in a position to proceed. Remember, the qualification process should determine not only if your product will serve their needs but whether or not they are financially qualified to own it.

We mentioned this in a previous chapter, but it pays to reiterate it here. When talking about financial matters, open the topic with the phrase *"Not to be personal, but . . ."* You're telling them that you know such things are considered private or personal. Yet you're still moving toward getting valuable information you need.

"In order to get your staff up to speed with this new software, there is some training recommended. What's your goal as to when you'd like everyone using it satisfactorily?" If your product requires training for the end users, that time frame needs to be addressed early on. You don't want a potential client to think using your software will be intuitive to their team. If you know it typically takes companies three months to master its use, you need to talk about those time frames during your qualifying sequence. This company may become disqualified if they need a faster solution or aren't able to put their people through training in a timely manner. Or, if they have staff in different locations, you may need to address multiple training days or training in an online format to get the job done in both a timely and an economical manner.

"Bill and Sue, if what we're offering sounds right to you, who other than yourselves would be involved in making a final decision?" Even if you're working with a married couple who appear financially sound, they may be relying on Grandma or Uncle Pete to finance a purchase. If

so, Grandma and Pete may need to be consulted before you can close the sale. You want to know this before you make a full presentation and try to close.

WHEN IT'S TIME TO WORK WITH MORE CLIENTS

If purchasing agent Polly places a smaller order than usual, you have every right to ask her some questions to find out why. Don't take it as an affront or that you're losing her business. It just may be time to qualify her for some new or changing needs.

Do yourself a favor, though, and ask your questions after the order is finalized. To do so beforehand might jeopardize the order. There's always a possibility that your client may take offense to your questions no matter how good you are at asking them.

It's important that you word your question so as not to sound like you're asking if something bad has happened at their company. Never say or do anything that could be interpreted as such. You're on their team and should be concerned about the welfare of their business. Your questions and comments should portray that.

"Thank you for your order, Polly. We appreciate your continued business. Now, typically, in the past, you have ordered in quantities of five thousand. Seeing that this is a smaller order, I'm curious what the reason is for that. Are your clients interested in something different, or are you feeling the effects of the current business climate like so many other companies?" It could be that Polly is shopping elsewhere for some new items to offer her clients. If

that's the case, you want to be the first one to supply that need if you have the right products. Polly might not have thought about asking you for information on other products if Bill Competitor has gotten a foot in the door with something different. Or, Polly could be intentionally weaning herself from your products because they're no longer needed or she's found something more economical. You need to act on any of those situations quickly.

If Polly's company is feeling the effects of a negative change in the market or in her industry, you will want to talk with her about what's happening. If you don't already have a handle on it, seek out information from other sources on what's happening in her field, and see if you can provide any new ideas to assist her company.

If it looks like she'll be placing smaller orders for a while, you need to take a look at how that will impact your bottom line and possibly find another client to fill that gap. Your goal is always to help your clients while keeping your income at the same level or increasing.

If a situation arises where someone is ordering smaller quantities or less frequently, it's a good idea to ask for some quality introductions. If you have served their needs well to this point in time, they may feel bad about the impact their downturn has on you. This may cause them to feel somewhat obligated to help you with referrals since you've gone the extra mile for them when they needed it. Never just accept a lesser order from a client and wish them well. That's what average salespeople do. You are a Champion. You are always striving to find the best solution for all parties, including yourself.

QUALIFY ALL THE TIME

In challenging times, you may need to continually requalify existing clients. Fastco Manufacturing might be a good client when they're running three shifts each day. But with any change in their production, such as cutting out a shift, their needs may change . . . and your services may need to change as well.

If Carol's Cookie Cupboard is experiencing an increase in business, they may need more of what you are currently supplying them. Be considerate of their time—especially if their business is on the rise—but be prepared to ask questions. It's okay to take a walk down memory lane to your initial sale with clients to see if their needs have changed.

"Carol, when you invested in your first two commercial-grade ovens from our company, you had just moved into this space. Now look at you! You've expanded into another part of the building. You have three new bakers on staff and are offering free delivery. Aren't you proud of this accomplishment? I'm curious—with how well your business is growing, how soon do you think you'll have a need for a third oven?" It could very well be that Carol hadn't given it a thought in all the busy-ness of her days. When you bring it up, she just might realize how much more efficient they could be with a third oven and conclude that it's time to expand her cooking facilities now.

ELIMINATING MONEY CONCERNS

One of the single best things a proper qualification process accomplishes is to eliminate money objections from coming up later in the sale. While I caution about bringing up the money too soon in a presentation—before you've had an opportunity to build value—it's wise to get a ballpark figure each client is expecting to invest in resolving their needs. You are bound to find potential clients with absolutely no idea how much services such as yours cost. They may have grossly underestimated what their financial position needs to be in order to make a purchase.

You can handle the money issue several ways. You can ask what type of research they've done on similar products. With so much information available online anymore, it's highly unlikely that you'll encounter clients with absolutely no idea of the investment range for your products, but it does happen. Besides, if your product has several models at drastically different investments, you'll want to know what level of investment they were looking at.

When they mention a particular model, you should briefly summarize the features. Then tell them how much it is in general terms. *"That model includes _____ and has a base investment of $_____."* If it's more than they expected, they will likely tell you. If they don't balk at that investment, ask questions about the features and benefits available on the next best model for their needs. There could be something there they missed in their research and might expect on the lesser model. *"The X+ model also includes_____; what that does for you is _____. Is that something you would find useful?"*

Another way to bring up the money is to talk about your other clients. *"Patty, many of our satisfied clients have invested as much as five thousand dollars for our products. Other, more fortunate clients have invested over seventy-five hundred dollars, and there are those happy clients who are on a somewhat limited budget. They typically have invested around three thousand dollars with us. May I ask which level do you think you'd be most comfortable with?"* Isn't that so much better than asking, *"So, how much money do you plan on spending?"*

Once you have a ballpark figure from them, you will know which products to present, and you've just eliminated a possible price objection later. They can't come back and say it costs too much when they've already told you they anticipated investing that much or more.

Do you see the power in a proper qualification process now? This is why it's the key to success for the Champion salespeople of the world.

SUMMARY

- Qualifying is the step in the selling process that makes the biggest difference in your sales volume.
- By qualifying properly, your potential clients will tell you what they want to own.

- You have a list of criteria of what makes a good, qualified client for your product.
- You know several ways to ask clients when they need the solution and how much they expect to spend.
- You have a plan for how to treat potentially qualified clients when you meet them in nonbusiness situations.

8. Reducing Sales Resistance

Half the worry in the world is caused by people trying to make decisions before they have sufficient knowledge on which to base a decision.

—Dean Hawkes

Worry is such a wasted emotion. It kills time. It depletes your energy. It interferes with your sleep and negatively impacts your productivity. Who would consciously choose such a thing? Not many of us, if we really thought about it. However, worry for most of us is an unconscious reaction to things in our lives. It has become a habit.

The phrase you typically hear is "I found myself worrying about . . ." *Found yourself?* It sounds like worriers are people who have gotten lost. If that's you, let's fix that.

The best cure for worry is the Serenity Prayer: *"God grant me the serenity to accept the things I cannot change; courage to change the things I can; and wisdom to know the difference."* If you find yourself worried about something ask yourself this question: *Is there anything I can do to change what I'm worried about?* If there is, take action in that direction—even if your first action is just to learn more about whatever is causing the worry, or even just to write down the worry and what you can do about it.

If there is nothing you can do about it, tell yourself out loud, "Stop wasting time and energy worrying." I know this sounds oversimplified, but if you will give it some thought I think you'll agree that it makes a lot of sense. And if you practice that little strategy repeatedly for a month, you'll find yourself worrying less and accomplishing more. Studies have shown that for chronic worriers 90 percent of what they worry about never happens. Some people would see that as an argument *to* worry: "Gosh, if I worry about that, it probably won't ever happen." Investing your "worry time" in taking action instead is so much more positive and will more likely bring you a positive end result.

Now let's look at how worry affects what you're trying to do in selling situations. It's an important element to be aware of. Your potential clients worry about making good decisions. They worry about whether or not the product will do what you say it will do. They worry about losing face if they make a bad decision. They worry about making financial commitments. All these worries may not be conscious to your client, but they're there and they're creating a thing called sales resistance.

Resistance to "being sold" is most likely the number one cause of lost sales for the average salesperson. They don't give a whole lot of thought to it or prepare to address it during their contacts with clients. Those average salespeople will likely tell you of experiences where they've hit a brick wall when trying to persuade potential clients to invest in their products or services. And, unfortunately, they have looked at that brick wall as an impenetrable obstacle to sales. They may try to push at it for a while, but rarely do they give thought or effort to scaling it, going around it, or opening a door in that wall—or at the very least a window (of opportunity).

Champion sales professionals understand that walls of sales resistance come down the same way they go up—one brick at a time. Though they may build very quickly, it's still a process that, once understood, can be slowed down or even stopped.

Let's begin with the foundation of that wall of sales resistance. You are a salesperson. You and they both know it's your job to move your product from your inventory to theirs. Thus, most people are generally resistant to salespeople. That's why we've covered so many strategies early in this book to help potential clients see you as friendly, helpful, competent, and trustworthy. All of those traits help break down that wall of resistance.

If you doubt that people are naturally resistant to salespeople, think about how many times you have said or heard these words: *"No thanks. We're just looking."* That phrase is the standard for putting off a salesperson when you're just browsing or for keeping your buying needs to yourself. In some cases it's said because people just don't want to talk with us. That's due to an old but unfortunate stereotype about salespeople being somewhat less than professional and only being in the job to push products on us. In reality, everyone works to make money, whether in sales or in any other field, but it's the salespeople who have caught the bad rap for decades because of the shady practices of a small percentage of those in this particular field.

Very few clients will agree to invest time with you if they already have a ten-foot-high wall of sales resistance built. You'll never reach them. So the fact that you have confirmed a time to talk with someone (or if they've come into your retail establishment) tells you there is some interest in your offering, a need—and possibly that window of opportunity. Your job is to keep that window open. It's not to lay the bricks of a higher and more solid wall, but rather to help your clients see that there's no need for a wall at all. You help them envision this new reality through education.

The core of selling is educating others. That's why so many teachers have successfully made the transition from teaching to sales. They have been trained to capture the attention of a class, pique their curiosity, and help them master their subject matter in an engaging way. When knowledge is gained, confidence goes up, and the desire and ability to make decisions on a subject increases dramatically.

Think about it. How did you approach the purchase of your first computer? If you were just excited to be getting one, you may have made a quick decision just to get it in your hands. But were you happy with it in the long run? Maybe. Maybe not. If not, what happened when you decided to upgrade? You sought out education. You asked trusted friends, relatives, and associates for advice and recommendations. You may have done some comparison research online. You may even have shopped around, seeking the lowest investment or the best after-sale service. The knowledge gained from that stage of the purchasing cycle gave you the confidence you needed to make what you considered to be a wise buying decision. That's how most consumers operate.

Your goal as a salesperson is to be the educator of your clients. You want to be viewed as a trusted advisor. You need to demonstrate that you have the knowledge to make a competent comparison between your brand and that of your competition. And you need to be accurate in knowing the current investments available for yours and similar products from other sources. This takes work—time and effort—on your part. Since you're a dedicated sales professional, it should be second nature for you to operate this way.

BRICK BY BRICK

We've covered that the foundation of sales resistance is a fear of "being sold." That fear will remain with your potential clients until you win them over, and they recognize you as a good and trustworthy person and your product as a wonderful solution for their needs.

A wall of sales resistance is rarely built instantaneously. It goes up layer by layer. Initially, every client makes a judgment about you, the person. Some do it consciously. For others, their initial reaction to you is subconscious.

If you come across to them as generally appealing that's good, but be aware that they still have that foundation of fear. If your clothing or appearance is unkempt or unprofessional, you've just laid the first row of bricks in their wall of sales resistance. If you fail to make good eye contact, have a firm handshake, or smile, more rows go up.

If you talk more to one member of the potential client team, committee, or couple than the others, more bricks are laid. Though when this happens, your wall may not be quite so solid. If the party you're directing more of your presentation to is the favorable party, the wall might now start to build unevenly. However, it's still a wall. If the opposite is true and you're giving more attention to a party who doesn't have as much influence in the final decision, your wall just got taller. Those extra bricks were added by the party who is feeling snubbed. While you're ignoring them, they're busy building that wall. Giving equal attention to all parties is very important.

The key is to understand that everything you do and say matters when attempting to reduce sales resistance or to keep it at bay. Your initial efforts at getting people to like you, trust you, and want to listen to you are critical to the shape and size of any wall of sales resistance.

We already discussed likability in an earlier chapter. Being likable begins with your smile, your tone of voice, your welcoming demeanor, your professional approach. It also involves coming across with an attitude of servitude. Your job as a sales professional is to serve the needs of others, remember? Make certain you do everything possible to transmit that attitude, and you will limit the number of bricks your potential clients will initially use.

So how do you build trust? Begin with clearly demonstrating the following sentence: *"I'm here for you."* If it weren't for clients you wouldn't have the job, right? Be appreciative of the time you're sharing with each and every client. It's more than a pleasantry. It's part of your job description—a requirement.

Another aspect of trust building (as opposed to wall building) is to find something you have in common with your potential clients besides this meeting. Human beings want to be around and work with others with whom they're comfortable. These are people we have something in common with. We may live in the same neighborhood, work at the same business, have children around the same ages, attend the same conferences, enjoy local professional sporting teams, or belong to the same clubs.

You don't find this out by giving your life history or providing your personal résumé to your clients. It's not up to them to find the common ground. It's up to you. You find it first with your eyes. How is their office or home decorated? If there's a particular style, ask if they chose it themselves. If so, make a positive comment about something in the room. Ask a question about something to get them talking about it. Then, you start seeking common ground with your ears. Their tone of voice and what they say should give you a clue as to something you might have in common.

If you find this difficult to do, treat them as an expert in something you've always been interested in (if it's true). Perhaps Bob Jackson is a fly-fishing enthusiast who has some photos and perhaps an antique fly rod on his office wall. You may never have done any fishing in your life, but you can start a conversation with *"How did you get started fly-fishing?"* or *"How long have you been a fly-fishing enthusiast?"* I would caution against asking where his favorite fishing place is. He may get suspicious that you want to tell others about his prime spot.

Do you see how easy it is to hand someone a brick for that wall of sales resistance? It doesn't even have to be anything directly related to the sale. Some offhand, seemingly harmless remark you make may turn out to be not only a brick but another bag of mortar to hold that wall together. That's why it's so important that you do your homework and prepare, prepare, prepare, for every client meeting.

Sue and Jerry Fellows may have a pair of quads or a camping trailer in their driveway. Unless you also see photos of them enjoying the outdoors together, don't assume they do. It could be that those outdoor hobbies belong to Jerry and his buddies, and Sue gets left at home or chooses not to go. Either way, those quads and campers could be bricks. You'd be better off looking for some other common ground first, such as telling them how lovely their home is, or talking about the people who referred you to these nice folks. As your conversations progress with them, you'll likely get a better feel for their enthusiasm for outdoor adventures.

Do your best to avoid the weather as a common topic unless there's something truly unusual going on. That's the lazy salesperson's way. It just doesn't have the polish of so many other potential topics.

Also, in case you've never heard it, avoid controversial

topics. Don't start a meeting with someone new by talking politics, religion, or about negative current affairs.

At the time I'm writing this book, the catchphrase for everything bad in our world is "It's the economy." I'm so sick of hearing that. That phrase, that excuse for people having challenges in their personal and business lives, irks me to no end. Just as we sales professionals are in the people business, it's the people of the locality, country, or world who make things happen. The "economy" is not some great external force that's making any of us do things we don't want to do. I'm going to take my own advice here and not go into the politics involved, rather focus on the personal level. Granted, there are some folks who are being downsized because of things beyond their control, but any suffering they feel because of it is due more to their lack of saving for that inevitable rainy day than anything else. Some of the people of the world are suffering financially or otherwise due to bad past decisions they've made. It's personal and they can blame no one but the person whose face they see in the mirror every morning.

Too many of us became greedy and took risks, and we weren't prepared when they didn't pan out. Rather than admit we got in over our

> *heads, we're now blaming sources outside our-*
> *selves and begging the government to fix it. The*
> *famous humorist Will Rogers had a saying for*
> *tough situations:* "If stupidity got us into this
> mess, why can't it get us out?"
>
> *If you find yourself standing in a deep hole*
> *of something ugly, before you expect someone*
> *to toss you a safety net please think about how*
> *you got there and what you can do to save*
> *yourself. Accountability is a predominant*
> *trait in people who are truly successful for a*
> *lifetime.*

Understand that the tone you start any client contact with sets the stage for the next few steps in the selling process. You want that tone to be warm and friendly—conducive to an enjoyable meeting. It needs to be solution-centered, as well. No matter how bad the situation that your client is facing might be, you're there to help them make things better. They did the right thing to call you or accept your contact. Meeting with you should be anticipated as a move in the right direction.

Other potential bricks in the great wall of sales resistance will come along as you move into your presentation. Your presentation materials must be in good order. Brochures don't have any fold marks in the wrong places, tears, or poor printing. Your laptop is clean. The desktop of your computer is uncluttered. In fact, all you should have on it are links to the materials you will use with this particular presentation. Your background is simple and nondistracting.

You may think this is silly, but if you have your favorite photo of your loved ones on your computer screen as most people do, it could be a negative for your potential client.

If you have a beautiful baby and they are childless . . .

If you enjoyed a wonderful vacation at the beach and they haven't had a vacation in years . . .

If you're holding a beer in your hand and they're firmly against alcohol consumption . . .

Do nothing—absolutely nothing—that could turn them off to what you have to say or distract them from your presentation. Any distractions should be created by you only for very specific reasons related to the sale of your product or service. You want them to want to listen to you, remember? If you're there and focused entirely on serving their needs, they will. Every second their emotions can change based on what they see or hear. We want to prevent any negative emotions and create only positive ones.

Let's take a look at what you will be presenting to your potential clients. If you have a standard presentation and choose to skip over a few points that don't apply to John and Mary Consumer or Sara the purchasing agent, you may make them wonder why they're seeing it or what they're missing. It's always better to have a minimal presentation prepared and to have additional information available at your fingertips if you determine it's appropriate when you get deeper into their needs. People are usually okay with you adding information as it pertains to the conversation, but they tend to become suspicious if content that is right there in front of them is skipped over or not explained. Any doubts that are raised during their education process can cause them to worry, second-guess themselves, and hold off making a decision.

How you handle any objections or concerns raised by potential clients also has an impact on their sales resistance. Concerns are not always bricks. Please don't assume they are. Most are simply requests for clarification. Your clients need a better understanding of one point or another. Some are offered up by potential clients just to slow down the buying process a bit and to allow them to rationalize the decision they're feeling compelled to make. If you change your demeanor when you hear an objection and become more aggressive or argumentative, you'll be handing your clients bricks and wielding the cement trowel yourself. Don't ever go on the defensive when you hear an objection. Simply see it as a request for more information. The calmer you handle objections, the more likely they'll stay on an even emotional keel, as well.

Other potential bricks are technical malfunctions during your demonstration, asking a closing question too soon, mispronouncing or misspelling names, cracking inappropriate jokes or making jokes at the wrong time, and asking personal questions in a blunt manner.

By incorporating the positive strategies covered in this book, you'll constantly work at bringing down that wall of resistance. Some strategies bring down only one or two bricks. Others will take down whole sections.

Think of it as a game. Can you remove bricks faster than they put them up? Or are you doing and saying things to help them strengthen that wall instead? When you work at the highest level of professionalism, there will be so few bricks available that the wall of sales resistance will become nonexistent between you and your clients. In fact, you both should soon find yourselves on the same side.

POOR DECISION MAKERS

When you have to make a choice and don't make it, that in itself is a choice.
—William James

It's bound to happen that you'll encounter some folks during your sales career who are just poor decision makers. It's sad, but true that millions of people go through life not making decisions at all or making bad decisions quite frequently. While it's impossible to make wise decisions all the time, there are people who are so afraid of taking on the responsibility of decision making that they let others run their lives for them. Some folks are so afraid to make the wrong decision that they will avoid situations where they have to do it. How sad to let the course of your life be decided by others—to go along with the crowd rather than step out and respond to life as an individual.

If you're in business-to-business sales, hopefully, you won't encounter too many purchasing agents with poor decision-making skills. After all, making wise decisions for their companies is their job. However, we won't assume that will be the case 100 percent of the time. Some of my students have told tales of purchasing agents who had very odd ways of making decisions. Others have encountered folks who put unbelievable demands on the salesperson in order to gain their business and still others who were very close to criminal in their activities as purchasing representatives. It happens.

Try as you may, you're not going to be successful with every potential client. Some will go to the competition even when you know in your heart of hearts that your product is the better choice for them. They simply don't have the same passion for it as you do. In some cases, they may weigh their analysis between products on different criteria than you are used to. Or they may not see the value in certain features that are the highlight of your product.

If a purchasing agent makes what you believe to be a poor decision, take the loss of business with grace. Wish them well and get their permission to touch base every now and then. If you are right in your evaluation of the situation, eventually they'll see the error of their ways. You'll want to be waiting in the wings for that day when they contact you for the better product or service (though don't hold your breath that it'll be anytime soon). Be careful never to gloat over being right if and when they come back to you. Just be appreciative of this new opportunity and honored to be able to serve their needs.

If the decision was a really bad one, you may be contacted by a new purchasing agent for that company. If you are, realize you need to build that relationship as if it's an entirely new contact, even though you may feel you have some type of history with the company. New purchasing agents are likely to find themselves in the position of cleaning up someone else's mess. You don't want to announce that you were any part of that mess—even if you never got them involved with your product.

Also, never knock the previous person in that position. For all you know, they moved up and still can influence whether or not you get the business. If asked about the previous contact person, stay neutral. Don't allow yourself to be put on the spot. You can use phrases such as, *"She had an interesting way of making decisions."* Or, *"It appeared that he worked hard at the job."* Stay noncommittal and you won't have to worry about the type of impression you make on someone new.

Whether you're working with a business or with consumers, these decision makers want to feel confident about their choices, be happy with the benefits of the products and services they choose, and to receive excellent service after the sale. Everything you say and do during your presentations needs to reflect that's exactly what will happen. You may even interject into your presentation comments such as:

"Doesn't that feature of the product make you feel better about our discussion today?"

"Mary, does that information cover your concern about . . . ?"

"You must feel better about your situation now that you see the great potential for improvement, don't you?"

"It's wise of you to do such in-depth research into this product line."

"Doesn't it feel good to have your needs so clearly outlined?"

"Aren't you glad we're analyzing this today?"

Those questions and statements are meant to make your clients feel good about meeting with you and learning what you have to offer as it relates to their needs. Your job is not just about the product, it's about the feelings generated within your decision makers. It's about the mental picture of things being better than they were before the decision was made—before they met you. It's about the end result of the decision making them more comfortable than where they are today.

People will take a lot of actions when they're uncomfortable. As a whole, we all want to be somewhere comfortable, no matter whether it's physical or mental comfort. When we experience any type of pain, our minds automatically start thinking of things we can do to reduce the pain, if not eliminate it altogether. Only when change is forced upon us or determined to be a requirement we hadn't anticipated do we think of it as painful.

The pain of change is one of the four demotivators I teach people to overcome. This may surprise you, but all you need to do to overcome any painful change in your life is to look at the reason you are choosing to make the change. What are you trying to accomplish? How will you feel once you have done it? If the end result of the change, your goal, excites you to own it, then it becomes something you have to have. When you have to have something, not having it becomes the painful thing. The pain of change has shifted to being a pain of staying the same.

Learn to apply that strategy to your decision makers, and you'll soon find yourself with more happy clients who are very comfortable with your product and your service.

WHAT ARE CLIENTS AFRAID OF?

During challenging times, you will have to work harder and be more patient with potential clients who are stalling decisions because of fear. During one of the bleakest times in American history, President Franklin D. Roosevelt put it best when he said, *"The only thing we have to fear is fear itself."*

Fear can be quite paralyzing. Consider the reality of what happens to deer when they find themselves blinded by the headlights of an oncoming vehicle. Because of fear, they react by doing nothing. If they would just move in any direction, the driver of the vehicle would naturally compensate by moving in the opposite direction and achieve a much happier ending for both animal and human.

When someone is afraid of making a decision you'll find them responding with stalls such as: *"I want to sleep on* it." "*I want to think it over.*" "*I need to take this to the committee.*" (Even when you've never been told there is one.) "*I'm going to wait thirty days, sixty days, or even three months to make a decision.*" "*Let me call you back on this.*" "*I want to run my decision by someone else.*" "*I'm just not ready to decide.*" "*I want to do a little more research before making a decision.*" "*I want to shop around.*"

When you hear anything along those lines from your potential clients your job becomes one of getting to the bottom of the fear. If your sales job is starting to sound more like the job for a psychologist, you're right in many respects. There are so many nuances to this business that I will be writing about them for the rest of my life and still may not cover them all.

So what are your clients afraid of? We talked about the fears of making a bad decision and losing face. But you have to consider the specifics of each client and their situation.

Are John and Mary fearful of committing $200 a month to a mobile phone service and a two-year service agreement? What if another reputable company offers a better plan after they've made the commitment? How will they feel? What will they do?

Is Bill worried that if he makes a decision to order five thousand widgets (because that gives him the best unit cost) then the market will slow down and he'll be stuck with them for years?

While we all know that no one can predict the future, we as sales professionals must do our best to paint a positive picture of satisfaction for our clients once they own our products. Again, we always keep in mind what's truly good for the client. We do not want them coming to us in a month or so saying, "I never should have made that decision." Even though it was their decision, they may hold a bit of a grudge against you because you were a party to it. You could lose their long-term business, their respect, and any referral business you might have gained if the initial decision truly was good for them. You may even need to say something like this during your presentations: *"Bob and Sally, no one can predict what the future will bring. The solution we've been discussing here today is to resolve today's challenges. I wish I could see sixty or ninety days down the road and make a recommendation based on that future, but I can only help you with the needs you've expressed here today."*

Some clients' fears will be so strong that you may need to present several scenarios for them based on what may happen in the future. *"If the future is bright, then this would be the best solution." "If things get worse, then the better choice would be . . ."* Then present the best solution for today, which should be somewhere in the middle. Most people will opt for that middle choice.

If you believe a client is just trying to stall making a decision, you'll need to employ some strategies for getting them off the fence. Here are a few questions to ask:

"When do you think you'll be ready to make a decision if not today?" Hopefully, you found this out during the qualification step of your sales cycle, but if not, you certainly want the answer now.

"What do you think might be different in thirty days that would affect your choice of solutions?" Maybe it's the start of a new fiscal year. Maybe they have a big sale of their own waiting in the wings. If it comes through, they have the finances to make the purchase. If it doesn't, they don't. The potential client might not feel comfortable disclosing this to you, but you do have the right to ask the question if you've done a good job to this point.

"When does the committee meet next? I'd be happy to make a presentation to them so I could answer any questions they might have." Never, never let a potential client present your offering to others involved in the decision. You always want to do whatever you can to present directly. That way you can watch their responses to your offering and answer any questions they might have. If you don't do this, the next conversation you have with this person will be *"Yeah, I gave So-and-so all the details and we decided it's not right for us."* At the very least get their agreement to present something that you prepare yourself. Be certain to cover all the details discussed in your meeting with this person so nothing will be left out. Then, your only challenge will be whether or not the others will actually read through it in depth.

If your potential client wants to shop around or do some cost comparisons, say this: *"Knowing the industry as I do, I'd be happy to assist you with any additional research or cost comparison you feel is necessary before making a decision."* Position yourself as an aide to him or her—someone who can help them accomplish the task more easily, more effectively, or in a shorter time frame.

With those questions and statements, you're in effect calling their bluff. If they're just stalling, it'll become blatantly obvious. If there truly is a need to wait on the decision, you want to gather as much information as possible about why, who is involved, and what other information they feel is necessary so you can stay in the game. You would never leave a client after hearing a stall without getting something else from them. Otherwise, you might as well hold the door open for the competition to come in as you make your exit.

Your goal is to get to the bottom of their fears. What's the real reason holding them back? Could it be that they just don't have the money and don't want to admit it? If that's the case, does your company offer short-term financing? Monthly investments? Would your company consider making a small initial shipment if there was a commitment in three months for the balance of the minimum requirement for orders? You are always looking for solutions. They must fall within the parameters of what your company can or is willing to do, but always be looking for answers to even the smallest aspect of the sale that could build resistance to the point where you do not get their business.

SUMMARY

- You have learned a method for keeping worry under control.
- You envision sales resistance as a brick wall. You know how bricks get added and how to keep them from being added.
- Everything you say and do is so you can have clients who like you, trust you, and want to listen to you.
- You recognize decision-making stalls and know how to respond to them.
- You help your clients see that only today's challenges can be resolved today.

9. Converting Clients from the Competition

During up cycles in your industry, there may be more than enough clients for your products, so you go after the easy business before approaching someone who is working with the competition. However, there will always be those larger accounts worth the effort.

In slow economic times there may not be as many people making decisions about owning your products. This means getting new clients to leave the competition will be an important option for you to consider. Strategies for getting clients to consider you over the competition will need to be employed.

> *Business is a good game—lots of competition and a minimum of rules. You keep score with money.*
> —Nolan Bushnell

When times are good and you have a trendy or innovative product to offer, you won't have to be overly concerned about the competition. The general feeling will be that there's plenty of business to be had. You won't feel like you're running in a pack—competing for sales. In other words, you (or your company) will be the lead dog in your environment, and most of your concerns will be about serving the clients you have and those who are seeking you out. It's a wonderful place to be, and I certainly hope you experience that situation many times in your selling career.

It's when you're not the lead dog that you have to look not only forward but sideways and back over your shoulders to see what everyone else is doing to gain their share of the market. That's when you will find yourself occasionally operating on high adrenaline levels, strategizing with others in your company to gain the business of key clients, and analyzing the competition's offerings to the nth degree. Believe me, those times can be very exciting and challenging—in a good way—if you have the right attitude about competition.

As an example, one of my students worked in a very competitive territory. He and one other competitor seemed to be going after much of the same business. It was frustrating him to find a company with the right qualifications for his product, only to learn that Mr. Competitor had already visited them and had gained their business.

Rather than let the competition gnaw at him in a negative way, he decided to meet him head-on. He found out the name of the competitor, tracked down his photo on his company Web site, and printed it out. He kept that other salesperson's photo in his pocket every working day thereafter.

Don't worry . . . this story doesn't have a weird or sad

ending. My student used that photo as a motivator. Whenever he felt like sleeping in, he'd think about that other guy. When he felt like quitting for the day, he'd reach into his pocket and look that other salesperson in the eye. He knew this person was good at his job and that he needed to keep working if he was going to claim a strong share of that territory for his company.

How do you respond when you learn that your competition is vying for the same client you are? Does it irritate you? Do you try to talk your potential client out of doing business with that other company? Do you knock the competition? Or does the thought of competition motivate you to step up and do a better job for the client? Do you strive to outshine the other guy to gain the potential client's trust and their business?

As you will have guessed by this stage of the book, the better road is always the high road. Never, never, never knock the competition! Don't do it with clients. Don't do it with fellow sales associates. Don't even think it when you're all alone. It gets you nowhere. None of your vital selling energy should be wasted on such a thing.

Knowing that you have competition should be a great motivator for you and nothing else. It should motivate you to play at the top of your game all the time. It should motivate you to make that extra call each day. It should motivate you to be innovative in your approach—to be different. Remember, in selling, different is good. Different helps you to stand out from all the rest of the salespeople your clients encounter. Different gets you remembered. By being different you will soon find yourself getting in the door with potential clients ahead of your competition.

As we mentioned in an earlier chapter, there will always be times when the competition faces challenges and goes out of business. You never want to be in a position of having to work side by side with someone you may have bad-mouthed to a client in the past. And, vice versa, you don't want to have to find a job with a competing company you previously spoke negatively about when your employer goes out of business. If you always take the high road, there will be nothing that might come back to bite you.

So, back to that high road. What *do* you do about the competition? First, you learn as much about their products, services, and ways of doing business as you know about your own company. Don't balk at this. If you're truly dedicated to your selling career, your industry, and your desire to serve your clients well, you'll find this knowledge readily available and more useful than you can imagine.

Unless you're a serious type A personality, you don't need to do this all at once. Just start paying attention to tidbits of information about the competition that come your way on a daily basis. I suggest you keep a notebook or file in your computer for each competing company. Record the information you learn about them there so you can easily find it when you need it. You'll soon find that you understand a lot about their products and how they compare to your offerings. You'll understand how they operate and see the differences (hopefully better differences) your company has to offer. This knowledge will help you structure better presentations of your own products. Your greater understanding will help you clarify key differences in the minds of your potential clients.

You see, your company and your competition may be in the same industry and go after the same types of clients, but you may not have your product information set up in such a way that it's easy for potential clients to make apples-to-apples comparisons. It's critical to your success that you know how both products measure up when viewed side by side and can demonstrate that to your clients. You may even have to walk them through the competition's explanations of their products in order to help them make the translation clear. They may think they're doing a simple comparison, but you may know it's more complicated than that. Confusion in the mind of a potential client is a sales killer. Don't let that happen to you.

When making comparisons with a competing company's products, you want to use their marketing materials, and their specs, or an independent source. If you create your own comparisons making up charts and graphs and so on, you may do a beautiful job but your client may wonder if you've skewed any information in your favor. If you show them how to read the competition's product specifications right from their printed brochure or Web site and compare it to yours, it's so much stronger.

ANTICIPATE THE COMPETITION OBJECTION

There's no denying that you have competition out there. There's no ignoring them, either. In going back to my comment about being different, I recommend that you anticipate your potential client's desire to shop around, to try to find the same or similar product from the competition. To do anything less is ridiculous. In fact, you should be the one to bring up the subject of the competition. I'm not crazy. Waiting hopefully for the conclusion of a sale without having to deal with the thought of competition is what's crazy.

Since you know that discussing a competitor's product is inevitable, prepare for it, bring it up yourself, and handle it smoothly. This puts you in control of the subject. It won't be something the potential client can use later in your selling sequence to stall the sale.

After you've done your homework about the competition, you will be able to say this to your next potential client: *"Mr. Butler, we know we're not the only company offering this type of product to people like you. We also know you might consider doing some comparison shopping as to the product specifications and investments. Because of that, it's part of my job to know as much about the competition's products as our own. All that research can be quite time-consuming. To save you some time, I'd be happy to help you with an apples-to-apples product comparison. Which brand would you be most likely to consider other than ours?"* There will be a few die-hard shoppers who will want to do their own comparisons. However, many will be glad to listen to you. After all, they've invested their precious time talking with you to this point. They are aware that you're an industry expert, and they now know it's your job to understand your product line across the industry.

When it comes to making buying decisions, most people want as much factual knowledge as is practical and to get the decision made—then move on to enjoying the product's benefits. If you can provide a one-stop experience for them to get their self-required due diligence done and have proven yourself trustworthy, why wouldn't they take advantage of it?

A fellow sales trainer and coauthor of mine, Laura Laaman, teaches a strategy she calls Shutting Down the Competition. She says:

"A great way to uncover any other options a customer might be considering is by memorizing and rehearsing the following question and stating it in a friendly manner: *'Barry, what other options and/or companies are you considering that I can compare and contrast for you today?'* Many salespeople don't ask such questions because they are afraid that by asking, they are telling the customer that there are other options, and the customer might end up choosing the competition. If your product or service is like most, your customer would have to be living in a cave to not know that there are other companies that attempt to offer the same product or service that you do. By dealing with this matter-of-factly up front, and offering to compare and contrast the differences for your customer, you are saving your customer time and letting them know that you have nothing to hide.

"Once you have uncovered other companies or options your customer is considering, have a prepared positive response to explain how your product or service is superior. Also, let them know that your option will be more or less expensive than the other option being considered. Memorize and rehearse: *'During our brief time together, I'm happy to compare and contrast the many differences, show you why this model is superior—especially in your situation—and why we are going to be a bit (more/less) expensive.'* This way they can be listening during your presentation to why they should buy your product and not wondering about those other points.

"Take the time to list five to ten ways that you are superior to other companies. What benefits or services do you offer that the competition does not? Is it free support, longer warranties, free replacement parts, quicker delivery, more exposure? During your time together, show them why your product or service is worth the investment. Make the differences clear.

"When done properly and nondefensively, your customers will find this approach refreshing and often reward you with their business."

Once a client gives you a brand or model they'd compare with yours, ask a few questions about why they chose that one. It might be that they saw some advertising for that brand. Maybe they have past experience with other products in that brand's line. Or, it could have been recommended to them by a trusted friend or relative who may have purchased the type of product they're now considering.

You need to tread lightly here. Not only do you not knock the competition, you never knock the advice your potential client has been given by someone else. Instead, it's your job to educate them and let them draw their own conclusions for their individual needs. Never indicate that the referring person made a poor decision or wasn't well informed. Remember those bricks from the last chapter? Handle this situation poorly and you will find yourself back to building that wall of sales resistance. Or, worse, you could be adding a very nice window of opportunity to the wall—one for the competition to get through.

If your potential client hasn't yet determined which of the competitor's products would compare to yours, say this: *"Many of our satisfied clients compared our current model to the XYZ Company's 200 Series models. What they found was . . ."* Give a brief summary comparison based on your knowledge of their products. Then, introduce a testimonial from a client who is happy with the decision to own your product over that other brand.

Know that the competition is always sitting silently in the corner when you are having discussions with any potential clients. Rather than let that competitor be a distraction to the sale, invite them to the party. After all, when you are the one in front of the client, it's your party. You get to decide how it goes. If you really know your stuff, the competition's information should be the catalyst that drives the client toward your product.

WHEN AN EXISTING CLIENT CONSIDERS THE COMPETITION

You're calling on Barb Crandall, the purchasing agent for Numero Uno, your biggest client. It's a standard contact. You're checking to see how things are going at the company and to confirm her next order. Barb is as friendly as ever, but when it comes to order time, she hesitates. She's told you the company has seen a downturn in business, but she didn't indicate whether it would affect your business relationship. If alarm bells are not already going off in your head, they should be. You need to test the waters to find out if something else has changed, such as Barb's need for your product or her loyalty to your brand.

"I'm sorry to hear that your company is facing some of those same industry challenges that are affecting others. It sounds like you're making some good decisions that should help get you through the current challenges, though. Your company provides a good service and should have a large enough market to survive some rough times."

"Thanks, we're a little nervous about our sales lately and need to be extra cautious."

"That's understandable. One thing you can always count on is us. We're ready to help you in any way we can. Will you be making changes in your order this month or do you have enough business on the books that it will stay the same?"

"Well, because of the changes going on, we've decided to take a look at some new opportunities with regard to all of our suppliers."

Slam! Most salespeople would have been totally blind-sided by this conversation. They would have stammered an *"Oh, I see."* Then, they may not have really listened to anything else Barb had to say. Instead, they're hearing the sound of their paycheck dwindling because they're losing this account.

Sales pros, when hit by news such as this, respond as if they're sailing a boat. Rather than let this news take the wind out of their sails, they simply take another tack and keep moving forward to learn as much as possible about what brought this change about. Until you know what caused the change in thinking, you won't be able to counter its effect.

If you have truly served this client to the best of your ability and your product has been satisfactory, you have the right to ask a lot of questions. If the quality of either your service or your product has lessened, you may deserve to suffer any changes that are on the horizon.

Let's take the former situation, where you've been on top of your game with this client. If you're given the well-earned opportunity, what questions do you ask? First of all, you don't want to go on the defensive. That would make you sound like a whiny child instead of a seasoned professional. Rather, be direct and assertive in requesting information. Information is your lifeline to keeping Numero Uno as a client.

If your purchasing agent tells you the company is thinking about researching new suppliers, you want to keep yourself on that list. In fact, you should offer to assist them with their research. After all, you're an industry expert and already know more than Barb does about the competition and their products. Be assumptive here. *"When things change like they are for your company, it makes sense to take a fresh look at outside services. What products or companies do you have in mind?"*

"Well, we're already talking with another company. In fact, we asked them for a proposal so I'm going to hold off on our next order with you."

"I see. Barb, not only do I work for Ultimate Products but I do my best to keep tabs on what's going on with the competition. Because of that I have a lot of information about other products and services that are available, including their product investments. I know you've already spoken with someone else, but why not let me help you with your comparisons? After all, I know your company's needs pretty well by now. In fact, if you'll tell me which company and product you're considering, I'll be happy to run a comparison for you with our product, which you're already using successfully. There are other, more economical choices out there, but you know as well as I do that your clients expect a certain level of quality from you. Let me help you evaluate your options. I may be able to come up with some minor changes you could make in quality that make enough of an impact on your bottom line to help you through the challenges you're currently facing."

When she agrees, you have your work cut out for you. But if this is one of your key accounts, it'll be worth it. Of course, your goal is to help them see that staying with you is the best course of action. Perhaps you have a lesser-quality product of your own they could switch to temporarily. Or, when you talk with your manager, something may be done as far as keeping their large-quantity discounts on smaller orders for a short span of time to help them through. You will find yourself being very creative about the possibilities once you're given the opportunity. Your job is to get that opportunity by saying the right things.

If the competition truly has gotten their foot in the door with one of your clients, remain calm and handle the situation with tact and grace. Hopefully, you truly have stayed informed on what the competition has to offer. If you haven't, it's now time to study their product's pluses and minuses.

Next, you need to review your history with this client. Refresh your mind on how well you've served them over time. You are not going to recite dates, facts, and figures of your history with them like you're building a legal case, but you want to be standing on solid ground with your information. Being able to refer to specific incidents where your personal knowledge benefited them will be important. You see, they aren't just considering doing business with another company and trying another product. They're considering replacing you with another salesperson. It could be they aren't thinking about how they'd be giving up your personal expertise if a new sales rep is handling their needs. When a company chooses your product or service, they don't just choose the company, they choose you. You are a very critical element and hopefully a valuable enough one that the risk of losing you is a consideration.

It's important to act before the client gets emotionally

involved with a new salesperson, their product, and their company. Remember our discussion of how people buy emotionally then defend purchases rationally? You need to get in there before their emotions start to change. Ask for an opportunity to visit with them in person, if feasible, to discuss their changing needs. Face-to-face is always best. Second best would be a phone meeting.

As I already mentioned, don't act like you're scrambling for their business. You are an industry expert at their service. You need to come across as such and help them see the value in your continued service to their company.

If you get the impression your client is leaning toward the competition, suggest they take caution in making a change. Suggest they check references and talk with clients who are currently using the other company's services. You do this out of concern *for them*—not just out of concern that you're losing them.

If the client does decide to make a change, this is where *grace* comes in. Don't burn any bridges. Don't act as if you think they're making a big mistake. Just get permission to stay in touch with them during the transition. Your actions all stem from care and concern for them. You want to be the one serving their needs, but if they choose to switch to someone else, you want to be certain they end up happy. If they are not happy, you'll be right there standing in the wings to provide them with an exceptional level of service once again.

I strongly advise you to get in touch with any lost clients within thirty to sixty days after they make the change. It's great if you can reach them directly, but even if you must leave a message on their voice mail, here's what to say: *"Barb, this is Tom. I'm just calling to see how things are going for you with the new product/service. As you know, I'm a stickler for your satisfaction. If you're happy that you made the change, wonderful! If you have any reservations whatsoever, know that I'm always ready and willing to assist you with further research or to serve your needs again myself."*

Believe me that this happens: longtime clients make changes they believe are for the better, then a few weeks or months down the road realize they were better off with you. Your attitude of servitude will help them find their way back to you. Any other attitude from you will cause them to get the feeling they'll lose face or have to eat crow if they do come back to you. If you keep their emotional state in the forefront of your mind, you'll find yourself acting more like the father of the biblical prodigal son—celebrating their return with a joy so great that they, too, are excited about it. Keeping in touch and following up can get you the client's business back from the competition.

GAINING BUSINESS *FROM* THE COMPETITION

So, how do you get a foot in the door with a company or an individual that's being served by the competition? First, you operate on the three Ps. You are Pleasant, Professional, and Persistent in all your contacts with your potential new clients. If you don't master the first two Ps, the third one won't matter.

You can't expect anyone who is working with the competition to jump ship and do business with you just because you contacted them once. There may be some cases where your competitor has not served their needs well and they are just waiting for a catalyst to make a change, but don't expect that to be the norm.

In most cases, your first contact will earn you a quick reply: *"Thanks but no thanks."* Your goal on an initial contact is not to sell anything, but to get them talking. So, never call to present your offer. Call with questions. If calling a business, ask the receptionist who is responsible for decisions regarding your type of product. Then ask to be put through to that person. If calling a consumer (assuming you're not violating any Do Not Call restrictions), ask how they make decisions about services such as yours. Remember, questions that make them think and get them talking are what you need to use during your initial contact.

If your product is landscape maintenance, parking lot cleaning, or janitorial services, you might say, *"Hello, Mr. Matthews, my name is Tom Hopkins. I understand you are responsible for decisions regarding the first impression your facility makes on your potential clients."* Never say, *"I hear you are in charge of the janitors."* Everything you say ties back to emotions. Mr. Matthews might be in charge of the janitors, but the end result of a job well done is that the company's clients receive a positive first impression. While most of us will quickly recognize the level of cleanliness of a building, we rarely notice the man or woman with the spray bottle, rag, and mop making it so.

When trying to get your foot in the door with a competitor's client, knowledge is your greatest power tool. Your knowledge of the competition's products and methods of doing business will help you start conversations with their clients. *"I know you're currently purchasing your supplies from the Green Company. Which of their products do you use the most—HandiSani or Clean & Clear?"* By mentioning products by name, you are demonstrating that you know your stuff. You know those products, how well they work, and how much better or more economical yours are.

With your early contact you mainly want to get a dialog going and get permission to get in touch again. Depending on your offering you may want to send them a free sample to use and compare to their current supplies. If your product is intangible, ask for permission to send them information that compares your product to the competition's, or tells about your exciting new offering or program. Once you have that dialog established, it may take only one more contact to get this client to consider your products. Or it may take seven or eight more contacts. When trying to knock John or Jane Competitor out of their spot, you need to take small but critical chunks out of their foundation, not try to destroy it in one fell swoop. Finesse your way into the offices, living rooms, and hearts of the competition's clients. Don't storm the doors!

Initially the potential client might think of you as nothing more than a bother. You'll hear things like, *"We're not interested." "We're happy with our current situation." "We're not making any changes."* That's okay. Think back to our chapter on objections. View these statements as nothing more than stalls. They just don't know you well enough yet to know how much they need you.

Remember that persistence is the key. As long as you are pleasant and professional, there's no reason for them to flat out dismiss you when you demonstrate persistence. Your persistence should create little doubts in their minds about the competitor's level of service. If that salesperson contacts clients rarely, they may find they enjoy all the attention you are lavishing on them. You want them to like you. Then you work on building their trust by saying you'll do something, then doing it. Once trust is earned, they'll want to listen to you.

Here are some words to use for some of the most common stalls you'll hear. The idea is just to keep the process moving forward—toward the next point of communication, contact, or discussion.

1. *"We're not interested."*

"I'm not surprised to hear you say that, Ms. Kelly. After all, you've been with ThatCorp for quite some time. They must be doing an excellent job of serving your needs. However, as you are well aware, we live in a world of change. All I'm asking is that you keep an open mind to the possibility of receiving the same or better service at a lower investment. Most of my clients switched to our service for just that reason and are so happy they did. May I at least have your permission to send you a sample / send information / contact you again in the future?"

If they agree to let you stay in touch with them, you've piqued their curiosity. Your communication may cause the client to contact their current provider to ask some pointed questions about not getting to them first with the latest industry information or free samples or whatever—and hopefully put that other company in the hot seat.

2. *"We're happy with our current situation."*

"That's good to hear, Gary. Would you mind sharing with me just what they've done for you that you enjoyed the most?"

"Well, I really like our salesperson. He sends us a lot of helpful information."

"Is the information specific to your needs, or is it general information about the industry?"

"It's general—like a newsletter. But I really get a lot out of it."

"Great, Gary. I'm curious: how long have you been a client of ABC Industries?"

"About five years now."

"Five years. And, how was the decision made to go with them?"

"Well, our other supplier was raising their prices so we decided to shop around. We checked out two other companies and went with ABC because they had the best price."

"Let me ask you—since you were able to benefit so much from comparison shopping before, doesn't it make sense to at least consider doing it again?"

Building to that last statement is powerful. It really gets them thinking about how much better they might be doing. When they agree that it's worth considering, the door is open. Do your job.

3. *"We're not making any changes."*

"I understand. It can be quite a daunting task to do the proper amount of research necessary to make a wise decision. I'm curious—if you were to consider making any changes in your program, what would you most like to improve?"

For some people, change is just hard. You'll need to get them talking to find out why they're so resistant. It could be that they had a bad past experience with some sweet-talking salesperson. It could be they're too busy to think about it right now, but thirty days from now might be a reasonable time to reconnect with them. Rather than trying to force change, get them thinking about some small dissatisfaction they have with their current vendor. This goes back to our discussion about the pain of change. Your goal is to get them to want to change because they realize they are uncomfortable with something now.

If you're going to try to sway someone your way from a competitor's product or service, then you need to get to the cause of their satisfaction or their dissatisfaction. Even if they're 100 percent satisfied with their current situation, you should be able to leave them with a positive impression—one that might bring you to mind for some referral business. Or, it might bring you their business should something change with the other company or salesperson very shortly down the road. It's happened that clients were satisfied with a product. Then the company moved the salesperson to another territory (or another position), and the clients just didn't get along with the new salesperson.

Changes were made not because of unhappiness with the product itself but with the experience they were having.

As the quote at the beginning of this chapter says, there aren't a lot of rules in business. You have a lot of freedom to explore possible ways to win over clients from the competition. Get creative!

SUMMARY

- Know the competition's products as well as you know your own.
- Use competition as a motivator.
- Be prepared to translate a competitor's information in order to fairly compare it to your own.
- You know what to do when an existing client considers the competition's products.
- You understand how to get your foot in the door with a competitor's client.

10. Closes That Help Clients Overcome Fear

No passion so effectually robs the mind of all its powers of acting and reasoning as fear.

—Edmund Burke

Fear is a mind robber. I think we can all admit that it's tough to make decisions when you're fearful—even if what you fear doesn't have anything to do with the decision. When times are challenging or even downright tough, you need to calm your own fears about what's going on before you can effectively help others.

If you're operating on fear that you won't make the sale, that you'll lose your job, that your company will go out of business, or that your industry will take a dive, you won't behave in the professional manner needed to serve your clients' needs. Once you calm yourself by realizing that all you have is this moment in time, this client (with needs you can serve), and the fine product you offer, you'll be ready to help your potential clients deal with their own fears.

What are their fears? Well, financial loss is a big one.

During times of uncertainty, people lean toward frugality. They try to hang onto their money a bit tighter or a bit longer. They don't make very liberal or expansive purchasing decisions. They're not all that excited about new things unless those things save them money or free up a lot of their time. They may fear long-term commitments. They're more likely to make buying decisions very similar to what they've always done. It takes longer to build trust with them because they're skeptical of nearly everything. With some people, it's almost as if there's a real-life boogeyman chasing them down. They're afraid to consider any type of change.

If the daily news is negative overall—covering layoffs, bankruptcies, business closings and so on—you can expect to encounter clients delaying purchasing decisions out of general fear. The news doesn't have to be about your industry, your products, or even their industry. If what they're reading, seeing, and hearing creates a fear mentality, you need to be prepared to work with it.

With the strategies we'll cover in this chapter, you'll help your clients focus on their current needs and the resolutions to those needs, then to take positive action to make their lives or businesses better. Envision yourself as an agent of positive change. You're a superhero of sorts who evaluates situations and helps people make wise decisions. You ease their fears and get them acting to make things better for themselves and their businesses.

When you encounter potential clients who initiate conversations with fears about current economic or industry conditions, you'll want to control the tone of your meeting by saying something like this, *"Brad, with all the negative news going on around us, doesn't it feel good to know that you're doing something positive by considering change?"* A statement like that sets the stage for the rest of your conversations with those clients. It's like you're saying, "Enough of that negativity. Let's get productive!"

True professionals find ways to use whatever is going on to make things happen. Negative feelings turn positive when good decisions are made. Past mistakes lead to wiser decisions in the future. Floods and hurricanes wreak havoc, but they also pull people together and help them plan better for the future. Nearly anything you see or hear can be turned into a powerful aid to closing sales. People love hearing stories (true ones) that help them see themselves coming out on top. Analogies also make excellent closing strategies. Become a master at using them!

WHEN DECISION MAKERS PROCRASTINATE

Potential clients may choose to procrastinate about making decisions when there's a shake-up in your particular industry. They may want to wait to see which players end up on top and which don't make the cut. While the waiting game might be wise in some instances, in others it does little more than delay a return to the positive side of the situation. The sooner people take action in a positive direction, the sooner those challenges will be overcome or fade away.

In times of industry disturbances, surprises about who will survive and who will not are rare. So much information about publicly held corporations is available that a quick analysis will usually provide enough information about the health of a company. So the waiting game can be eliminated as an excuse not to make a buying decision. If your industry is under fire and you work for a publicly held company, print out a copy of the latest balance sheet for your company and keep it with you. Proof that your company is healthy is bound to come in handy. And reading the latest news about your company should be the first thing you do every morning in order to prepare for questions or concerns your clients may have. Your potential clients probably are doing the same. Know what they're reading, seeing, and hearing about your company or your industry so you can counter that news appropriately.

When your decision makers do decide to procrastinate, you have two choices for how to handle them: (1) wait them out, which I don't recommend unless you know they have an approaching deadline for making the decision; or, (2) say and do the right things to get them moving. In other words, nudge them off the fence.

If you're a seasoned pro in the selling game you may not believe this next statement. Initially, you may not recognize that someone is procrastinating. Some people are very good at appearances. They may request additional information, analyze details in great depth, or attempt to arrange ideal scenarios for meetings. It appears they're moving forward, when in reality they're simply spinning in place.

Once you realize what's happening, you need to ask some questions. Ask the procrastinators to summarize for you what they're thinking. Have them clarify the pros and cons of your offering as they understand them. Listen for something you can get hold of and work with. It could be that they have misunderstood an important benefit of going with your product. It could be you left a piece of information that's vital to their decision out of your presentation. Getting to the root of what's holding them back is critical.

It could be that they truly don't have enough information yet to make what they would consider a wise decision. It can be hard for a client to admit they don't know enough about something to make a decision. It's an uncomfortable feeling, especially after they've had it explained to them so well by this nice salesperson. However, once they tell you what's holding them back it can be an easy fix, can't it? You just put your educator's hat back on and go to work.

Another strategy for working with procrastinators is to create a sense of urgency in making the decision. Is there a chance of a price increase for your product anytime soon? Say these words: *"I understand your hesitation to make the purchase today, Carol. However, waiting until next week may not be in your best interests. The investment quoted today is only valid through this week. Knowing you'll save quite a bit, don't you think it's wise to make your decision now?"*

How about a supply shortage? *"Jim, I understand your thinking about ordering just enough inventory for these displays, but what happens when that sells out? Don't you think it's wise to order some back stock now rather than hope we'll still have the sizes and colors you'll want when these are gone?"*

Does your decision maker have a specific install date in mind that requires them to order so many days in advance? *"Mr. Collins, there's a manufacturing period of forty-five days for this equipment. If you need it installed on the fifteenth of next month as you indicated, the order must be placed no later than today."*

Is your product one such as investments, where the longer you have to allow the money to accrue the better? Is it insurance that is best to put in place sooner than later? Try saying something like this: *"Katy, Will, the sooner you make this decision, the sooner your family will be protected in the case of an unfortunate circumstance."* Granted, that plays a little on the guilt side of things, but if they have agreed to everything up to this point and you know the product is truly good for them, they may need that type of nudge to put their approval on the paperwork. Wouldn't you hate yourself if you didn't nudge them, letting them postpone a decision, and something *did* happen?

When attempting to nudge a procrastinator, their best interest has to outweigh any discomfort you may feel. Of course you wouldn't cross the line to becoming aggressive in any way, but some people don't respond well to subtlety. They need to be asked very direct and pointed closing questions.

Others can be nudged with an assumptive close. If they haven't come right out and said no to your offer, keep moving forward to the close. Then say, *"Patty, if you have no other questions or concerns about how well our product will serve your needs, all that's needed is your approval on the paperwork right here."* Now, Patty has to do something, doesn't she? She either approves the paperwork or gives you a reason why she won't. Either way, you're moving forward—either with the delivery of the product, or the delivery of more information to solidify your case that your product solves her needs.

CATCH ME, CATCH ME

Perhaps your decision makers have had a rough go of it lately, either personally or in business, and are simply enjoying all the attention you're giving them. Some people find the pursuit part of the sales process quite flattering. They may not be ready to give up the chase.

Your job with these folks is to explain to them how well you serve your clients after the sale. Describe the level of service you give in detail. Ask how and how often they want to be contacted. Promise to do just that. You may need to go so far as to arrange an "after-purchase" meeting even before the decision is made. Of course this can always be changed if they don't make a decision, but your willingness to schedule time with them in advance of knowing for sure about the sale should ease their concern about being courted less after the sale is made. It's wise to help potential clients see the added benefits for those who become clients—even if it's not something specific to the product, but just you giving them more of your time and attention.

For example, if your product requires installation or training, assure them that you'll be there every step of the way. Lay out a schedule, if you must, of what each step entails and when it will be happening, who is involved, and the time required. Eventually they'll be on their own with the product. Let them know about scheduled follow-up visits and how they can reach you in between. Reassure, reassure, and reassure them that you're not going anywhere once the sale is complete. The sale is just the beginning of a long-term relationship.

IS THERE ENOUGH TRUST?

It could be that those making the decision just don't trust you enough. They may like what you have said, but not be 100 percent sure the benefits are as wonderful as you've presented them. You build their trust by listening attentively when they speak. Typical salespeople are so busy thinking about what they'll say next that they often miss important information relayed by potential clients. It can be a tough habit to break. So if you are like that, replace those thoughts with actions to help you focus on what they're saying. Visually and verbally let them know you're paying strict attention to what they have to say. You lean forward. You maintain good eye contact. You nod your head. All of these body-language signs tell them that you're with them—that you are following what they say—that you empathize with their situation and truly want to provide them with a good solution for their needs.

Don't overtalk. Too many salespeople talk their potential clients right out of sales by saying too much. It's almost like a nervous habit. They don't feel like they're in control unless they're talking. Read a crime novel and you'll see that the people who talk too much usually have something to hide. You don't want your potential clients thinking that's what's going on with you.

You must be extremely courteous all the time, but know that courtesy will go even further with those who are fearful. Don't think this is a trite point. It's amazing the difference in feelings generated in potential clients when you say things like "please," "thank you," and "yes, sir" versus when you don't. Always err on the side of formality when it comes to common courtesies.

Being respectful of the potential client's time helps calm their fears. If you're taking too much of their time, they may fear the purchase will require them to add more work to their already busy days. If you don't invest enough time with them, they may feel the decision is not all that important. It's a balancing act, to say the least, and only by doing and then evaluating what you've done will you find just the right levels.

I'd suggest you consider saying something like this to help ease fears created by concerns about time: *"Mr. Casey, I will always be respectful of your time as our business relationship develops. I will contact you only as often as you would like and in whatever manner you desire. Your time is valuable, and I do not want to waste any of it on nonessential matters."* Never let a fear sit in the corner and send out negative vibes. Assume things like the value of time are important in every selling situation. You are demonstrating a high level of courtesy and professionalism by addressing it.

Some clients will need to receive weekly contact even if it's just a quick phone call. This will help allay any residual fears they may have after making the purchase decision. When they get more comfortable with you, your product, and your service, they'll likely require less attention.

CLOSES FOR CHALLENGING SITUATIONS

A sales close is nothing more than a way to ask for the order. Statistics have shown that most sales occur after five closing attempts. That means your clients know at least five ways to stall the sale or to say no. If you know only one or two ways to ask for the sale, how often are you likely to close?

True professionals in the sales arena have a large arsenal of closing strategies and are looking for new ones all the time. Having made sales my hobby many years ago, I still find myself analyzing selling situations I witness or am a party to. How did what that person said or do make me feel? Did I agree to give them my business? Was it a pleasant experience? How does that translate for other types of products or situations?

As I mentioned earlier, nearly any situation can be used to create a closing strategy. Some closes work better with consumer sales, others with business-to-business sales. I'll give you a few here that have been proven to work in both up and down economies. There are many more to be found in my other books and in the teachings of other sales trainers. I recommend some other trainers that I know are of a high caliber on my Web site. You'll find a link to Recommended Educational Products on the Free Resources page of my Web site.

Each strategy you choose to employ needs to be delivered with the true warmth and sincerity you feel for your clients. If you have read this far in the book and do not have those feelings for your potential clients, you need to consider another career. Selling is always about what's good for them.

Use these closing strategies until you get comfortable with creating your own.

The "I Can Get It Cheaper" Close

You would use this close when your potential client stalls you with wanting to shop around or look for a better bargain. Their fear is twofold. One fear is that they're making a bad decision. The other is that they will part with too much of their money for what they're gaining in benefits. You need to calm those emotional fears and help them rationalize the decision.

Start by agreeing with them. *"That may well be true, Jerry. And after all, in today's economy, we all want the most for our money. A truth that I have learned over the years is that the cheapest price is not always what we really want. Most people look for three things when making an investment: (1) the finest quality, (2) the best service, and (3) the lowest price. I have never yet found a company that could provide all three—the finest quality and the best service at the lowest price. I'm curious, Jerry— for your long-term happiness, which of those three would you be most willing to give up? Quality? Service? Or low price?"*

Rarely will clients want to skimp on quality or service.

What you've done here is reminded them—in a kind and gentle way—that you get what you pay for. This reinforces the benefits you've already been discussing as being of tremendous value and should put a little doubt in their minds about the level of quality and service they might get elsewhere when trying to save a few dollars.

The "Economic Truth" Close

You'll find this close useful in business-to-business situations. It's great for when your potential client is comparing you against the competition that you know offers a product inferior to yours. The client may be leaning toward their lower investment, but you know, based on their needs they'll be happier with your higher quality product. Once again their fear is of spending money unwisely. These words play right into that fear:

"Debbie, it's not always wise to guide our buying decisions by price alone. It's never recommended to invest too much for something. However, investing too little has its drawbacks as well.

"By spending too much, you lose a little money, but that's all. By spending too little, you risk more because the item you've purchased may not give you the satisfaction you were expecting. It's an economic truth that it's seldom possible to get the most by spending the least.

"In considering business with the least expensive supplier, it might be wise to add a little to your investment to cover the risk you're taking. If you agree with me on this point and are willing and able to invest a little more, why not get a superior product? After all, the inconve-

niences of an inferior product are difficult to forget. When you receive the benefits and satisfaction from the superior product, the investment, no matter how much, will soon be forgotten."

I know that one is kind of long, but it works. If you're nervous about memorizing it, break it down into small sections and work on the gist of it. Once you have some success with the concept, you will be more motivated to learn it to the point where it rolls smoothly off your tongue.

The "I Must Do" Close

This is a great one for procrastinators—people who just don't seem to want to make a decision but aren't giving you anything to grab onto. It's based on a time planning/productivity strategy I've taught for years. The strategy is simple. When you live by these twelve words—*I must do the most productive thing possible at every given moment*—you accomplish more in each day. That saying helps you gain clarity and focus on what's really important to be doing every minute of every day.

When you have clients who are spinning their wheels, say these words: *"I understand that you're hesitant to make a decision today, Sherry. You probably have a lot on your mind. I learned a saying from a speaker once that makes a lot of sense when it comes to handling business matters efficiently. The saying goes like this: 'I must do the most productive thing possible at every given moment.' Makes sense, doesn't it? It really helps you focus your efforts effectively. Now, let me ask you, what's the most productive thing you could be doing right now?"*

Don't be surprised if they try to change the subject by saying something like *"Laying on the beach in Hawaii."* Procrastinators are famous for trying to take the conversation off course. With an answer like that you would agree that rest and relaxation are important to productivity, but then guide them back to the reality of where they are right now.

If their answer has nothing to do with your meeting, such as finishing reading a report, meeting with their staff, getting the kids' soccer uniforms washed, or anything that could be a mental distraction, try these words: *"Okay, then let's get this decision out of the way so you can get on to something more productive."*

If the answer is to get this decision made, you would say, *"Good. Then we're handling just what you want to do right now. With your approval right here we'll welcome you to our happy family of satisfied clients."*

Either way, you're asking for the sale—now—and giving them a rational reason to make the decision. If they've already emotionally agreed that the product is right for them, this strategy is great for nudging them into getting the decision-making process behind them.

If the time frame from initial contact to the final closing question has been a long one, your client may temporarily feel at a loss when the project of finding a supplier is done. Our productivity statement helps them recognize the value of moving on to the next most important thing.

The "It's Not in the Budget" Close

When there's a lot of belt-tightening going on, people and businesses tend to watch their budgets very closely. You may hear "It's not in the budget" whether it's a consumer sale or a business situation. The important thing to remember is that a budget, like the economy, is not an entity unto itself. They are both created through the efforts and decisions of people.

Your goal when faced with a budget objection is to get to the heart of its true worth—why people create them and who makes decisions about how they're managed. Try these words: *"I understand your desire to work within your budget, Frank. I'm fully aware of the need for companies/people to have a good handle on where their money is going. Would you agree with me that your budget is a necessary tool for wise money management?"* They will, because they think it's stopping the progression of the sale and that you're giving up. But you're not. Next, you say, *"The tool itself doesn't dictate where the money goes. You, as its creator/manager, do that. A good budget has some flexibility built into it for emergencies, changing needs, and unexpected opportunities. You, as the controller of that budget, retain the right to make changes that are in your best interests (or the best interests of the company), don't you? What we've been discussing here today is a product that will allow you (or your family, or your business) to gain an immediate and continuing benefit. Tell me, under these conditions, will your budget flex? Or, will it dictate your actions?"*

You've just put them in the power position as controller of the budget. They will admit they could make changes. And, you've asked them to do just that in order to gain the benefits of your product.

If they stand by their budget your next question would be *"Then how do we get included in the budget?"* If they see the value of your offering and do want it, they'll consider what actions must be taken to make it so. They may say they need to make some adjustments that will take some time. If that's the only way you'll make the sale, agree to be patient but get a date from them as to when they expect the changes to occur. Get a confirmation to meet on or prior to that date. Be prepared to give a mini-presentation and summary recap of all the benefits to bring them emotionally back to wanting to own the product, then close the sale.

The *"Colin Powell"* Close

Here's a perfect example of taking something that was in the news and turning it into a close. During the Gulf War in the early 1990s Colin Powell was a general. If you follow him forward in history, he retired from the military and became our secretary of state. I would think most Americans are familiar with his name. One of his quotes from a military debriefing resounds wonderfully when you have a potential client who is simply indecisive. I turned it into a close.

"Kirk, I once heard a quote by former Secretary of State Colin Powell. It went like this: 'Indecision has cost Americans, American business, and the American government billions of dollars—far more than a wrong decision would have cost.' What we're talking about now is a decision, isn't it? What will happen if you say yes? And what will happen if you say no? If you say no, noth-

ing will happen and things will be the same tomorrow as they are today. If you say yes . . ." Then lead into a benefit summary. End the summary by saying, *"The sooner you make the decision, the sooner you will start enjoying all those benefits, won't you, Kirk?"* He'll likely agree and you then ask for his approval on the paperwork.

The "Competitive Edge" Close

No matter where you are on the economic cycle today, business clients will always be seeking ways to gain a competitive edge. If Business A thinks Business B is doing better than them, they'll want to take the same actions. This close brings that thought to their minds.

"Maria, please realize that your competitors are facing the same challenges today that you are. Isn't it interesting that when an entire industry is fighting the same forces, some companies do a better job of meeting those challenges than others? My entire objective here today has been to provide you with a method for gaining a competitive edge. And gaining edges, large or small, is how you can make this one of those few companies in your industry that is doing a better job. How soon will you want your company to start doing that better job?"

If you have a client in a noncompeting industry that has used your product to gain an edge, be certain to show this potential client their testimonial. Even better, ask the existing client if they would take calls from potential new clients in noncompeting industries to discuss how well your product (and you) have served their needs.

The "Negative Economy" Close

When the primary concern your clients are having is related to a negative or down economy, you may not be able to get their minds off it. With some people, rather than trying to convince them that the glass is half full, you need to agree with them that things aren't great. However, by using the words in this close you will get them to admit there are advantages to making decisions even in the worst economic times.

"Irene, Jack, I have to admit that I agree with you when you talk about the poor economic situation we are currently facing. However, years ago, I learned a very interesting truth. Successful people buy when everyone else is selling and sell when everyone else is buying. All we seem to hear lately is news about the bad economy, but I've decided not to let it bother me. Do you know why? Because many of today's fortunes were built during the tough economic times of the past. The people who built those fortunes focused on the long-term opportunity rather than the short-term challenges. You have that same opportunity here today. In looking at the long term benefits of our service, it just makes sense to get started now, doesn't it?"

You have just helped them once again to rationalize the decision they emotionally want to make.

The "In Today's Economy" Close

For potential clients who know they need to make a decision but are so caught up in what-ifs, try this close to help them to focus on their needs.

"Based on today's economic news, nearly everything is either too bad for us or too good to be true. If we take all the information presented to us each day to heart, we'll never buy anything. Our economy would grind to a halt and we'd all suffer greatly. You are in a position to make a positive choice for your family/company, don't you agree?"

When they agree that the choice is positive, ask for the business!

The "Business Productivity" Close

When businesses have been facing challenges, making cutbacks, and possibly laying off employees, decision makers can be kind of down in the dumps. If you market a product or service to businesses that either benefits their employees directly or that their people will use, take the focus off the decision and put in on the positive result. Try something like this: *"Wayne, what I am offering here today is not just a product/service. It's a boost in employee morale. Haven't you noticed that anything new increases job interest and excitement? Excitement increases morale. Morale increases productivity. And what is productivity worth?"*

This tactic works especially well with products such as health insurance, office equipment and furniture, vending machines, and services that impact employees' working environments.

Hopefully by now you see the pattern with the most effective closing strategies:

1. Agree with whatever the potential client is saying.
2. Turn them around with stories, questions, quotes, examples, testimonials.
3. Create a sense of urgency.
4. Act as if the decision is already made in favor of owning your product or service.
5. Ask clearly and directly for the sale.

This pattern will help you ease the fears of potential clients and get them off the fence.

SUMMARY

- You understand what the most common client fears are.
- You know how to recognize a procrastinator.
- You know how to create a sense of urgency about making a buying decision.
- You use strategies for building their trust in your word.
- You know and use proven, effective closing strategies.

11. Methods for Cutting Costs While Continuing to Appear Successful

It is not the strongest of the species that survives, nor the most intelligent, but the one most responsive to change.

—Charles Darwin

History has revealed to us many large, strong companies that did not survive challenging times well because they were resistant to change. Their lack of responsiveness to changing markets or business cycles caused them to suffer losses and invest valuable time and resources in recovery.

At the time of this book's publication, many of our nation's newspapers are struggling to reinvent themselves. While print media is still enjoyed by many, more and more people are getting their daily news online or from television. Technology has advanced to where we can be plugged in almost anywhere on the planet. While newspapers provide a valuable service, the "paper" part of the equation is costly to produce and distribute. It will be interesting to see how these news resources cut those costs and transform themselves.

Being forced to change can be painful in all sorts of ways when you resist it. It's much less painful when we embrace change, knowing that it's for our own good. As Darwin says, we must be responsive in order to survive.

For a company or a sales professional, change needs to be a choice. It needs to be a wise choice. Running willy-nilly and putting bandages on every little cut and scrape encountered during tough times is not an effective way of handling challenges. A better way is to get yourself out of the brambles altogether with well-thought-out moves toward efficiency and productivity.

Hopefully, you are prepared to weather the various business cycles and potential changes we covered early in this book. If you've taken care of critical business issues, then when the tide of change does occur you should be able to survive quite well with additional minor adaptations.

The hope is that none of the changes you need to make have a negative impact on the quality of products or service that your clients receive. In fact, I strongly suggest you temper every change considered with this question: *"How will this change affect those doing business with me?"* If the answer is *"It doesn't,"* wonderful! If it does, the next question is, *"Will it impact them enough that they may no longer wish to do business with me?"* You never want to put a change in place that causes this to happen, but there have been cases where it was necessary to do just that in order to save the business (or the career) in the long run.

Companies have been known to walk away from smaller clients in order to serve the needs of their larger bread-and-butter clients. Some small clients have demands or needs that are too costly to continue to meet. And they may not be able to afford your products or services if you need to increase pricing in order to make a decent profit.

It's always wise to analyze the percentage of profit coming in from each client and handle their needs accordingly. If you have a large profit margin on certain products that are in demand by smaller companies, it may be wise to downsize the amount of time you invest with your larger clients. Keep in mind that it's important to look at both bottom-line dollars and profit-margin percentages. You wouldn't want to lose a large account that generates high revenues for six small companies who have higher profit margins unless the bottom line dollars are there.

BELT-TIGHTENING TIPS FOR SALES PROS

When business slows, for whatever reason, you may need to tighten your belt a bit, both personally and in regard to how you spend your time and money for business. Start by becoming as efficient as possible. Then, if you still need to do more, consider where you spend your money. Track your spending for just one week and you may be surprised to see how many ways you can save if you adjust your thinking and your habits.

Though salespeople have the potential to earn much more than an average nine-to-five employee, they also have a tendency to want to spend. We want the latest and greatest gadgets. We like new cars. We enjoy traveling for both business and pleasure. I've said for many, many years that the easiest sale you can make is to another salesperson.

I myself own three vacuum cleaners that were sold by door-to-door salespeople. Even though I had two vacuums in the house already, I didn't have one that would suck a bowling ball out of the closet. And, boy, did I want that! Silly, isn't it? But the salesperson did such a good job I just couldn't turn him down. You see, as a sales professional myself, I know how rejection feels. I know how hard our jobs can be. I'm a soft touch. That's why I have a team of people who now make all the business decisions for my company. Typically, I'm a frugal guy, but when I see a good sales presentation, I want to own, whether I need the product or not.

If you're cut from the same mold I am, develop a strategy for your buying decisions and stick with it. This may involve consulting a loved one or business associate before making major purchases. You may limit your nonessential spending to a certain dollar amount for a while. Or, you may decide not to purchase any nonessentials until you've economized enough to justify it as a reward.

Develop an economy mind-set and keep it turned on all the time. You'll be amazed at how much you can improve.

As an example, consider your eating habits. Many people are quite surprised when they tally up their receipts for food-related expenses for a single week. Do you really need that thirty-two-ounce soda every afternoon? Would sixteen ounces suffice? The thirty-two-ounce size might be the better deal, but it still costs more than a smaller-sized drink. Are you supersizing your fast-food meals when a regular-sized one would save you both money and calories? Do you stop eating when your stomach is full, or do you always clean your plate?

Some of my students have developed the habit of halving their restaurant meals when they are brought to the table. They eat half and take the other half home for another meal later. By doing so, they just eliminated the cost of a whole meal! You don't need to make a big deal out of this or literally draw a line down the middle of your plate, but make a mental note and consider it the next time you order at a restaurant.

Also, I know how we salespeople like our coffee. The question then becomes, do we really need the fancy coffee drinks? If you're going from the coffee shop to the office, might it help save some money if you keep your own supply of coffee add-ins? Do you always order the extra-grande size? Take a look in your cup the next time you have one. Did you really drink to the last dregs? If not, next time order a smaller size and see if you really notice anything different besides the amount of change you get back from the purchase.

If you're an independent contractor, I strongly advise you to never eat alone! As sales professionals, we often find ourselves away from both the home and office at mealtimes. Don't just grab a quick bite. Take advantage of the tax deductions and the good will created when you have breakfast, lunch, or dinner with clients or potential clients. This may take a little advance planning, but it is well worth the savings.

For other terrific ideas about tax deductions for business, consult with my fellow trainer Sandy Botkin. He was formerly with the Internal Revenue Service and now works on the general public's side of the desk. He is very fun to listen to and has the IRS code backing everything he teaches.

I will caution you about cutting corners with your accounting or tax services. Unless that's your educational background, it's just too easy to mess up. Continue to work with professionals for these services as long as you have income and expenses to report. Their expertise should save you more in the long run than you would save by doing it yourself.

Now, let's take a look at your clothing. One of the perks of being a sales professional over doing manual labor is that you get to dress nicely. That was one of the aspects of sales that appealed to me when I was nineteen and working construction. When I worked as a bridge deck specialist carrying steel, some summer days it would take me two really long showers to get clean after working outdoors all day.

If your standard of dress for business is a suit, ask yourself if you can get along with what you have for another season. Can you update it with a new shirt, blouse, tie, scarf, or jewelry—something not as costly as a new suit? If you can, do it. If not, then, determine your budget, watch for sales, and shop wisely.

This is where purchasing classic styles of clothing is a good idea. As an example, President Barack Obama has been known to purchase five of the same suit once he finds one he likes well enough. It makes his choices simpler. That's economy of thought!

A friend of mine who is in the high-end jewelry business has chosen a uniform of sorts for his business attire. Whenever he's conducting business, he always dresses in a particular style that "suits" him and his position in the industry well. If you choose a "uniform" for business that's appropriate, don't worry about getting bored with it. Instead, realize the peace of mind and cost savings it can bring you. And, as mentioned above, you can always change things up economically with minor changes in jewelry or other accessories.

Are you or someone you know handy when it comes to making minor repairs on clothing? Consider repairing items over replacing them. As a whole if we become less of a throwaway society, it'll be better for our wallets and our planet.

If your position requires that you take clients places in your vehicle, it had better be in good condition. Never skimp on something this important. Having your car break down on the way to or from a client lunch—with the client in the car—is never a good thing. While keeping it in top running condition is a job for professionals, you can certainly handle the cosmetic details yourself. Rather than going to the car wash weekly, see if you can get by with wiping down the car with one of those soft cloths and wash the windows yourself. Even better, add cleaning the car to your kids' chore list and increase their allowances (but not as much as the professional car wash would be).

Has your briefcase taken a beating lately? If so, grab

some leather cleaner and see if you can resurrect it. Some people you will meet in business will be very judgmental. If anything about you shows a lack of care, untidiness, or disorganization, they may harbor doubts about how well you will handle their needs.

What do your shoes look like? Pay attention to them before you walk into a potential client's home or business. I know many guys who will notice dirt or dust on their shoes and do a quick wipe on the back of a pant leg. The challenge there is that now your pant leg is dirty and possibly noticeably so. Check your shoes before putting them on. A quick wipe with a rag can eliminate having to give them another thought for the rest of your day.

The same level of care needs to be taken with your laptop computer. If it looks like it's been through a war zone, consider getting an attractive cover for it. Keeping up appearances is important in this business. Clients want to do business with successful representatives of their industry. In tough times you may still be considered one of the highly successful ones, even if your sales are down considerably.

It's critical to keep yourself as educated as possible to serve their needs, but don't fear showing that you're making some cutbacks, as long as they don't affect the quality of service you provide. Your clients will respect you for being honest about things not going as well as in the past and appreciate your creativity in coping.

Now, let's get back to how else you can cope. What are you purchasing in office supplies? Are any of those items things that might be available from your company? If not, might they be more economical if you had a business account with the office supply store? Many of the larger chains offer rewards programs. It takes only a few minutes to join and can bring you some nice savings.

Can you make time to shop for bargain supplies, generic brands, or overstock items online? You might be quite surprised to find out what's available. Do you know someone who could help you with this? Perhaps there are other independent sale pros just like you who could form a buying group to save all of you on these types of expenses. Start asking around.

When it comes to your computer, consider whether or not you really need to print out as many documents as you do. As an example, more and more medical offices are going to paperless files for their patient information. Can you do the same? If you can't do it with every document, are there some you can keep as electronic files only?

My staff and I are seeing more and more e-mail messages arrive with a small statement at the bottom about saving paper by not printing the messages unless absolutely necessary. Think about how often you actually go back into paper files these days. Granted, it's nice to know that you have every document related to each client, but does it have to be a paper document? Does it have to take up physical space? Or will cyberspace suffice?

I'm a nut about proper grooming. It's so important to present ourselves professionally when our careers involve service to others. Don't cut any corners here that will affect your personal appearance. Granted, if you typically get a haircut every six weeks, maybe you could stretch it to seven weeks to save a few dollars, but only if absolutely necessary. And I know how women feel about getting their nails done. Yes, manicures and pedicures may have initially been a luxury but are likely to have become viewed as a necessity. If you feel that way about it, don't stop doing it. Even I will admit that there's a point where frugality, forced or not, just hurts the psyche. If you're going to be mentally depressed about making a cutback, it will show in your attitude and could very well negatively impact your closing ratios.

On the other side of the coin, you can't look at every strategy for belt tightening as too difficult to do. Hold yourself accountable for finding ways to cut back just 3 percent of your spending during a month's period of time. Once you manage that and realize that it's not too tough of a pinch, you'll find yourself developing a new habit of saying, "How much more can I do?" It'll become a fun game to see how and where you can make cuts that no one other than you notices.

Making a game out of economizing in your personal life can work well with your family. This is one of those things that you *can* do when faced with challenges. Taking action, rather than becoming immobilized by fear or indecision, helps you gain a sense of control over the situation.

If you must travel for your job, be certain to take advantage of every special offer, bonus, or reward program you can find. This may take a bit of doing to track, but if you treat your travel needs as well as you treat the needs of your clients, you'll find yourself enjoying almost as many benefits from your savings as rewards from serving your clients. Also some airlines offer Web-only specials on travel.

Most clients will understand if you must visit them in person a little less frequently than during high times. Of course some clients will need more attention. We already addressed that. For those who can do without the face-to-face contact, consider using online meeting services such as WebEx, Microsoft Live Meeting, or GoToMeeting, or simply meet with them via webcam. That way they can still see your smiling face, and you don't have to invest a whole day of travel (and the expense) to be there. If you don't already know how to use these services, schedule time into your calendar this week to learn. Ask other salespeople (or your favorite teen) for some basic instruction on how to take advantage of this technology.

If your client doesn't have a webcam, might an investment of less than a hundred dollars to send him one be more affordable than a plane ticket, rental car, and hotel to visit in person? And you could learn how to use them together. That's a great way to create a new bond or strengthen an existing one—thus building customer loyalty.

If you work from home, consider how much energy you can save. Some utility companies offer lower rates for business clients. Talk with yours to see if you qualify for that savings. Turn off lights, computers, printers, televisions, whatever, when you are not in the room. Switch light bulbs to lower-energy ones. If you're replacing appliances or equipment, seek out products with a quick return on investment. You might be surprised to learn that an average desktop workstation often costs more to power over the three years you'll use it than it costs to buy it. Spending a touch more for a low-energy model can pay off.

Invest a day analyzing the services you subscribe to. Is there a more economical plan for your mobile phone? How about your cable TV? Your insurance coverage? It's very easy to start these services and forget about them. Or to upgrade features without realizing that you don't really use them.

When paying bills, do so not just on time but early, whenever possible. Credit card companies will take as many as three days to log your payment, so your best bet is to pay soon after receiving your bill if you have the money in your account and can pay the balance in full. If you miss the closing date, you may be charged the larger of a late fee or interest on the old and new balances.

Hopefully at this point you're developing your own economy mind-set. Don't become a nervous Nellie every time you need to spend some money, but do pay more attention to where your money is going. Get out of the habit of swiping your credit card without looking at the total or checking the receipt. Just commit to adapting some common-sense strategies for keeping more of the money you work so hard to earn.

COST-CUTTING MEASURES FOR BUSINESSES

If you work in an office and rarely have clients as guests, you have more room for cost-cutting measures than a retail location where clients can drop by anytime during business hours. One of the best things you can do is to ask everyone who works in the office to look around and think of ways to cut expenses or improve client experiences. We have done this twice in our company history, and my team came up with ideas that truly helped us through some challenging times.

Another great resource is your suppliers. If you offer a physical product, could there be a more economical method of packaging it? Can your print materials be redesigned to use less paper or to save other printing or binding fees? Negotiate with all your suppliers. Trust me, they will be happy to help you save money if it means keeping your business for the long haul.

I know of an office where they cut their gardening service back from once a week to twice a month. They cut their janitorial service from three times per week to once a week. Occasionally, the office staff had to empty their own trash cans or refill the paper towels, but the savings made that little extra effort worthwhile. If you weren't in that building on a daily basis you'd probably never have noticed any difference in the levels of service they were receiving. In a retail situation, you might get away with cutting back the gardeners but certainly not the janitorial services. Do what's most appropriate for your situation. In fact, it's important to stay on top of all of your maintenance. This includes maintaining your heating and air-conditioning units, your computers, and your other office equipment. Skimping in this area might cause you some costly repairs or replacements when you least expect them.

Where I live in Arizona, I've noticed many retail shops have installed skylights. It's so sunny here that they have been able to reduce the amount of powered lighting required for their stores to be cheerfully bright. Others are switching the types of lighting they use to bulbs that require less power yet provide sufficient light for the type of work being done.

Some companies are changing their hours of service. Some are switching to longer hours but being open one day less each week. Some businesses couldn't survive closing one day a week, but there are others that manage just fine. Just be certain to notify your clients before making such changes and offer them an emergency number to call in case of a special need.

Take a look at any services that are outsourced. Is there something you're paying an outside consultant or service for that one of your employees could take on?

When it's time for cost-cutting measures, I recommend that you review the job descriptions of everyone on your staff. Also, review each person's strengths and weaknesses. If business is slow, is there someone who typically does data entry who could move over to making customer service calls to generate more business? How many hats can your people wear? What skills do they have that you're not maximizing? Can you put the talents of two people to work on a special project that would otherwise need to be outsourced? Not only would it save the company money, but it may reinvigorate those two staffers to work on something outside their normal scope of work. Being asked to try something new is usually a great boost to employee morale. It increases job interest and excitement. Excitement increases morale, and morale increases productivity. Even if your people don't have the skills or talents to take such a project to completion, if they get a good start on it, then you will pay an outside talent less to finesse it and wrap it up.

This next point may sound silly, but it's amazing what can come out of it. We were facing some cutbacks in our company. I started thinking about how much we spend on office supplies. Taking the better part of one morning, I searched for basic office supplies such as pens, adhesive notes, paper clips, and so on that were at my home. I was amazed at how much had accumulated in the various nooks and crannies. I was able to take a full lunch bag into our office and show my staff. While they laughed at old frugal Tom, it also inspired many of them to do the same and to get all our supplies centrally located in the building. With the amount of items found, we were able to cut our office supply budget that month. It wasn't so much the value of what was found but the exercise of organizing the supplies that made us all feel good about being just a little frugal. And taking action for the good of the company created a nice level of energy that I'm certain carried over to other aspects of our business.

During times of stagnation or recession, people understand that raises and bonuses will be impacted. They never like it, but they do understand. Most people will be grateful to still have jobs and not be too worried about a cost-of-living increase. If you can swing it, I recommend tying any increases to production. Perhaps pass along a percentage of expenditure savings if you put your people to the task of finding ways to cut costs without impacting service. Or share a percentage of increase in business with your people, if feasible. Most companies find that rewards tied to results are quite effective, and by tying them to both savings and earnings allows even your receptionist or accounting staff to participate. It's not all about the sales department.

I have heard of several companies and public institutions asking their employees to take some time off without pay in order to save some jobs overall. Most people are agreeable to doing this rather than seeing some of their coworkers lose their jobs entirely.

SHARING THE WEALTH (OR SAVINGS)

In challenging times, other than a personal sales slump, realize that whatever is happening is rarely something that's happening only to you. It's likely impacting other family members, your business associates, your neighbors, your clients, and your suppliers. At times you may feel like you're walking in a gray haze of uncertainty or downright gloom. You can't let it dominate your actions.

True professionals in every field of endeavor know that their positive actions are not only good for them, but that they are obligated to share what they learn with others. Be the ray of sunshine through the clouds. Always approach others with something positive to say, or a story about something you or someone else implemented that made a positive difference.

If in your field of selling you create resource lists or send out newsletters to your clients and potential clients, start sending a series of positive tips. You may even want to send them in the form of attractive cards or e-mails that your clients can share with others. The further the positive tips spread the better for all of us. Include details, if appropriate, on what each tip did for you or someone else. One word of caution: always get permission before talking about what someone else did.

SUMMARY

- Before making changes you consider how they will impact your clients.
- You analyze the value of each client to you and your company.
- You are developing an economy mind-set with regard to all your expenditures.
- You are committed to sharing your cost-cutting successes with others.

12. Selling Is Service

It is not the style of clothes one wears, neither the kind of automobile one drives, nor the amount of money one has in the bank, that counts. These mean nothing. It is simply service that measures success.

—George Washington Carver

The foundation of a successful career in selling must be the desire to serve the needs of others. Granted, most people choose the field of selling because they know there's good money to be made in it, but the money comes only after the service. In fact, I often tell my students to take the S in the word *Service* and change it to a dollar sign, like this: *$ervice.* That mental picture helps them understand that the income we receive is in direct proportion to the amount of service we give to others. It's a kind of scoreboard reflection of how well we do what we do.

Beware that if money ever becomes more important to you than the service you provide, you will stop making money because your reasons for being in sales will be wrong. You must be sincerely interested in the needs of others in order to become truly successful in selling.

Some people decide to "try" selling while waiting for their real careers to evolve, because it doesn't always require a great deal of higher education. When you only give something a try, you aren't likely to do as well with it as someone who is dedicated to it. Don't let the fact that it's pretty easy to get into sales of some sort or another allow you to think it's an easy business. My mentor, the late, great J. Douglas Edwards, used to say that selling is the highest-paid hard work and the lowest-paid easy work there is. If you aren't willing to work hard, don't expect to earn a very high income. Of course some areas require specific training or licensing, but many situations require only a good attitude (that *service* attitude) and the desire and ability to learn about the products being offered.

Some people start selling as youngsters and keep at it because it's all they know. I think everyone should take part in selling something at some point in their lives. The younger it's done the better. It forces you to communicate with other people. It challenges you to say and do the right things to achieve a successful outcome. It's excellent training for life itself. After all, we're all selling something.

We sell ourselves at our jobs daily—whether they're sales positions or not. When seeking new employment, we're selling the product we know best—ourselves and the skills we have developed. We sell our fun selves to our friends. We sell our loving selves to our family members. We sell our caring selves to our neighbors. We sell our ideas and values to our children or someone else's children over whom we have some influence.

The more we understand that every interaction we have with another human being is a sales situation, the more successful we become in life as a whole. Our goal with every situation then becomes one of coming up with a win-win for everyone involved, rather than a competition to see who comes out on top.

No matter how we got here, most of us stay in selling as a career because we enjoy how we feel when helping people and businesses make decisions to acquire or get involved with our products or services. Based on my conversations with students, I'd have to say that the level of job satisfaction in sales is consistently high even when the times are challenging.

I know I initially stayed in real estate sales because of the great satisfaction I enjoyed. I felt so good helping young families and some older folks—who had only dreamed of home ownership—decide to buy a home. Through my words and actions I helped them become educated enough to make wise decisions. I helped them to see that they could afford the American dream of home ownership. Later, it was seeing the light of understanding dawn on the faces of my students that kept me selling "selling skills"— something I still enjoy very much today.

There's a tremendous amount of personal fulfillment to be had in a well-managed selling career. I love to compare selling to the medical field. Like doctors, it's our job to analyze symptoms and make recommendations that lead to better health. The symptoms we address are the needs of our potential clients. Their health is a direct result of the benefits of our offerings. And like most doctors, we are well-paid for our knowledge, expertise, and service.

How many other careers are there on the planet where you get to help people buy something that will benefit them, receive monetary reward for doing it, and have them thank you at the end of the experience? Yes, if you're doing your job of service properly, while you are thanking them for their business, they'll be thanking you for helping them. That is the standing ovation of sales—a sincere thank-you from your clients after they've made a decision to own the benefits of your product or service. What's not to love about that?

People are better off for knowing us. Businesses perform their business functions better because of us. We make others look good. We make them feel good. We help them find ways to have more, be more, and do more with their lives and businesses. Selling is the greatest profession in the world!

SERVING THE MASSES

The profession of selling also helps satisfy our natural human curiosity about the world around us. We get to meet new people all the time. Even if our product has a relatively small potential audience, our attitude of servitude carries over into our lives. When we meet someone new we learn a little or a lot about their lives, depending upon the type of product or service we provide. And in most cases, we're better people for having known them. Their thoughts, dreams, and circumstances broaden our thinking beyond our own little corners of the world.

Once the mind is stretched by a new experience or a new understanding because of someone else's experience, it never shrinks back. We are ever-growing and expanding creatures, flourishing more than many of our human counterparts because of our chosen careers.

As sales professionals we get to experience the challenge of finding, educating, and persuading others. We exercise our creative muscles. We're constantly seeking out new connections, new ways of engaging people and building their curiosity to know more about our products and services. We serve their needs, not just with our products but with our experience, with the knowledge we gain from the experience of others and the connections we help them make.

Salespeople are little catalysts for the world—making things happen. If it weren't for us taking on the responsibilities of this profession, nothing would happen. People and companies that create products wouldn't know what to do to market them. People and companies with needs wouldn't be able to satisfy them. This all relates back to selling as a great and vital service to the world. Aren't you glad you've chosen it as a career?

SERVING YOUR OWN NEEDS

There may be times when you don't feel up to giving your finest service. That's to be expected. The important thing is that you realize you're not giving it your all and give the best you can at that moment. Make a mental or written note to go the extra mile at another time for any client who may receive less than your best today.

You see, your behavior at any given time is influenced by your opinion of yourself. If something is going on in your life where you don't think very highly of yourself, you may find it difficult to reach within for the strength to provide your highest level of service to your clients. Have faith in yourself. You can do anything you make up your mind to do. Once your mind is made up, you will find out how to do it and be willing to pay the price to learn how to do it well.

If you're having a tough time finding the energy to face the daily challenges of your selling career, it's time to take control of your thoughts. Thoughts lead to actions. If your thoughts are negative or fearful, you risk becoming less than you are capable of being. Why settle for less than you can be? You can't succeed when your mind is darkened by confusion or fear. Fear creates a resistance to change— and as we've covered throughout this book, change is the key ingredient for success. Start improving your attitude and your situation by realizing that unhappiness is a sign that you're ready for change. You are the architect of your own life. Nothing that has happened to bring you to this point in time matters anymore. The only thing you can control is the present moment. If you allow yourself to think that things won't get better, you are putting yourself into a mental prison. You will suffer a slow emotional death if you don't act.

At the very least, when you're down, do something different from your normal pattern. Get up at a different time of day. Go to bed at a different time. Eat breakfast before you shower rather than the other way around. Drive a different way to work. Park in a different parking spot than you usually do. By acting differently, your mind will come out of its autopilot funk. You will see things differently. New ideas are likely to come to you.

I heard a program on creativity once in which the trainers said to make a conscious effort when dressing first thing in the morning. If you typically put your socks on first, put them on last. If you put your left leg in your pants first, switch to the right. And so on. It sounded silly, but when I tried it I found it more challenging than expected. My conscious mind had to be activated to focus on completing the task. It did make me feel different than I did when dressing automatically while thinking about what the day would bring.

It's important to have balance in your selling career. You can't give, give, give to others all the time without running out of both physical and mental energy. That's why I strongly encourage you to work with a planner of some sort, and be certain to schedule nonsales activities on a regular basis. Even if you love your job and your family to no end, you need to love yourself as well. You demonstrate this by including healthy habits in your schedule— exercising, eating right, and taking time for quiet, relaxation, and renewal. Having a sense of balance will enhance the creativity you need to face challenging times.

NEGATE THE EFFECTS OF NEGATIVITY

Don't allow yourself to sink into negativity no matter what is going on in your world. Negativity is nothing more than a way to justify being average. It is a way of rationalizing why others might be doing better than you are. And what are we doing when we "rationalize"? We're buying that thinking. We're taking ownership of it. Don't let that happen to you.

Any time you feel anything less than positive and good about what you are doing, take a step back and ask when you gave yourself permission to be anything other than successful. Start guarding your mind against negative thoughts. Think about what you think about.

If you work around negative people, be conscious of how their attitudes affect yours. Limit the time you spend hearing what they have to say. In fact, strive to listen only to people who are doing better than you are—those who are like the person you want to become.

Not everyone who takes my training or reads my books becomes successful. That has always bothered me because the same information is available to everyone. I've often wondered why some take it to heart, and the next time I hear from them they tell me of how much they've improved their closing ratios and job satisfaction, while others we never hear from. I have had to accept that they were either looking for easy answers or were not truly dedicated to serving the needs of others.

If you now realize that you're not doing some things you should be doing, stop fooling yourself. Shed any masks you might be hiding behind. Shed your pride and admit that you can do better. Don't accept mediocrity.

You are the sum total of your choices. Becoming happier and more productive just means you'll be making different choices. You are successful when you enjoy your life and fulfill your potential. You have a unique combination of gifts and talents. Exploit them! Never give up on yourself.

Thomas Edison was once asked about his genius, he replied, *"Genius? Nothing! Sticking to it is the genius! . . . I've failed my way to success."* When you try something new, it may not work as well as you hope. Don't give up on it, though. Give yourself the benefit of the doubt. Ask yourself, *"What did I do right?"* First you tried something new. That was right. Then break down what you tried and find the parts and pieces of it that did work. For those that didn't work so well—consider how you might adapt them to make them work better for you.

TRAIN YOURSELF TO SUCCEED

During challenging times, it's more important than ever to dedicate yourself to training, practicing, and improving everything you do. Being well trained will help you be one of those people who thrives not just now but when things turn back around, as they always do. Don't just rely on your company to train you, either. The fact that you're reading this book tells me that you're self-motivated. That's good. Too many average salespeople try to blame the lack of training or motivation from an external source, such as the company, for their challenges. No one can motivate you but you. Others can hold you accountable but they can't change your attitude about what you do. They can't inject you with doses of ethics or enthusiasm. In the end, it's all up to you.

If, after reading all this material, you put the book aside and never look at it again, things will probably stay the same for you as they were before you read it. If staying the same makes you happy, that's okay. Be happy.

However, if you are not happy with where you are right now in life and with your career, keep this book on your desk or in your car or briefcase—somewhere easily accessible. Before each client contact flip through it and review just the phraseologies we've included. (Hopefully you took my early advice and read the book with a highlighter, adhesive notes, and flags.) If nothing else, the words I've taught you to use will get you thinking and speaking differently. You'll start saying things the way your clients want to hear them. You'll create mental pictures of ownership in their minds. You'll think of more and better ways to help your clients rationalize their decisions.

Each of us experiences abundance only to the degree we allow ourselves to do so. When you're worth more, you'll earn more. Keep finding ways to neutralize your natural resistance to change. Make yourself uncomfortable where you are and you'll take the steps necessary to get where you want to go. You can alter your life by altering your attitude.

Think about the mental picture you have of your life. If you aren't sure what it looks like, look around you. Your environment is a reflection of what you are thinking. If you don't like what you see, start to change by altering your mental picture of yourself, your career, and the life you would be happier living. If you were living your ideal life right now, what would a typical day look like? What type of room or bed would you wake up in each morning? What would you see when you looked into your closet and dresser drawers? How would you feel when you looked in the mirror? What type of nourishment would you provide your body? What kind of car would you drive? Take yourself through a whole day just picturing that day. When you have a clear image of it, all the way to when you lay yourself down at night, realize how satisfied you feel. Do this mental exercise several times each week and you'll keep that satisfied feeling. Soon you'll find yourself providing a level of service to your clients that brings you the life you see in your mental picture.

SUMMARY

- Money is a scoreboard reflection of the amount of service you give.
- We are constantly selling—ourselves, our ideas, our values, *and* our products.
- We grow in direct proportion to the number of people we meet and serve.
- We realize the necessity in serving our own needs as well as the needs of others.

Reference Material
(in order of appearance in the book)

p. xvi Tom Hopkins International, Inc. http://www.tom hopkins.com/

p. 5 John G. Miller. *QBQ! The Question Behind the Question.* http://www.qbq.com/

p. 35 Daily Activity Graph. http://www.tomhopkins.com/free_resources.html

p. 37 SendOutCards. http://www.tomhopkins.com/SOC contact/SOCcontact.html

p. 37 "Thank You Note Phraseology." http://www.tom hopkins.com/pdf/ThankYouNotePhraseology.pdf

p. 53 Henry Ford. http://en.wikipedia.org/wiki/Ford_Model_T

p. 65 Earl Nightingale. *Lead the Field.* http://www.night ingale.com/prod_detail.aspx?productidn=116

p. 74 Tom Hopkins. *How to Master the Art of Selling.* http://www.tomhopkins.com/mm5/merchant. mvc?Screen=PROD&Store_Code=T&Product_Code=1035&Category_Code=classics

p. 75 Dale Carnegie. *How to Win Friends and Influence People.* http://www.amazon.com/How-Win-Friends-Influence-People/dp/0671723650

p. 77   Tom Hopkins and Pat Leiby. *Sell It Today, Sell It Now.* http://www.tomhopkins.com/mm5/merchant.mvc? Screen=PROD&Store_Code=T&Product_Code= 1530&Category_Code=sales_closing

p. 91   Dan S. Kennedy. http://www.dankennedy.com/ index.php

p. 176 Laura Laaman. http://www.lauralaaman.com/

p. 216 Sandy Botkin. http://www.taxreductioninstitute .com/

INDEX

**BUSINESS
PLUS**

Recognized as one of the world's most prestigious business imprints, Business Plus specializes in publishing books that are on the cutting edge. Like you, to be successful we always strive to be ahead of the curve.

Business Plus titles encompass a wide range of books and interests—including important business management works, state-of-the-art personal financial advice, noteworthy narrative accounts, the latest in sales and marketing advice, individualized career guidance, and autobiographies of the key business leaders of our time.

Our philosophy is that business is truly global in every way, and that today's business reader is looking for books that are both entertaining and educational. To find out more about what we're publishing, please check out the Business Plus blog at:

www.businessplusblog.com